Pompey

Part Two
The Rock 'n' Roll Years
1960-1965

George East

Pompey Lad
Part Two
The Rock'n'Roll Years
1960-1965

Published by La Puce Publications

© George East 2022

website: www.george-east.net

Typesetting and design by Francesca Brooks

paperback edition ISBN 978-1-908747-82-2
kindle edition ISBN: 978-1-908747-83-9
e-Pub edition ISBN: 978-1-908747-84-6

Other books by George East

Just a Pompey Boy (1949 – 1955)
Pompey Lad Part One – Growing Pains 1954-1960
Rough Diamond
Home & Dry in France
René & Me
French Letters
French Flea Bites
French Cricket
French Kisses
French Lessons
French Impressions: *Brittany*
French Impressions: The Loire Valley
French Impressions: The Dordogne River
French Impressions: Lower Normandy
French Impressions: 150 Fabulous French Recipes
The Brittany Blogs
Home & Dry in Normandy (compilation)
French Kisses (compilation)
Love Letters to France
France and the French
A Balkan Summer
A Village in Bulgaria
A Year Behind Bars
How to write a Best-Seller
The Naked Truth about Women
The Naked Truth about Dieting

& the Mowgley Murder Mysteries:

Death Duty
Deadly Tide
Dead Money
Death á la Carte
Dead & Buried
The Kiss of Death

LA PUCE PUBLICATIONS
e-mail: lapucepublications@hotmail.co.uk.
website: www.george-east.net

This book is dedicated to my family, and the thousands of friends, acquaintances and even foes who touched my life during the years covered in this episode. Still with us or not, all influenced my past and future, whether for good or not-so-good. A sincere thanks to you all.

Author's Note

This is the third book in what was planned to be a series of one.

Pompey Lad II is mainly about life in Portsmouth at the dawn of the so-called Swinging Sixties. It's also about my chameleon-like transitions from motorbike-mad Rocker to would-be hard-nut Teddy Boy, pub gang member, scooter-riding Mod and cool James Bond-style man-about-Portsmouth.

As you will discover, my youthful escapades were perhaps a little extreme, but I think broadly similar to many young men and women at that exciting time. It was, of course, a time when society changed so dramatically from the grey post-war years to what seemed to many a new and exciting world.

Whether you believe The Sixties and what followed was a change for the better or worse will, I think, depend on your age, attitude and how much fun you had in those far-off days.

PS: Because of the truly vast quantities of beer, 'scrumpy' cider, acid (LSD), upper and downer pills and whacky baccy I ingested, my memories of the Sixties are understandably patchy in parts. I am thus grateful for the help of old friends, foes and lovers and in some cases, police and court records and arresting officers. Far too many too mention individually, but they know who they are. Specific acknowledgements and recommendation to where you can find out more about this period in Pompey's history are to be found at the end of the book.

Finally, in many if not most cases, names have been changed to save any embarrassment or legal or physical damage to me. This is particularly so in the case of female persons mentioned. If you are a lady who shared a fleeting moment of my life and recognise yourself in spite of the alias, thanks for all the memories - and (mostly) fun.

The Music of Life

The hit songs and tunes listed at the start of each year are just a selection of the hundreds that were the soundtrack to my life - and anyone else of about the same age. I've also included snatches of some of the lyrics that worked their way into millions of heads and hearts and stayed there forever.

Bite-size Pompey

For those who've not had the pleasure of acquaintance with our fair city and to set the scene for the forthcoming action, here's a snapshot of Pompey's past and present:

- Emerging from coastal marshlands at the end of the 11th century, Portsmouth became the nation's premier naval port because of location and the foresight of monarchs and military leaders going back as far as the Roman Occupation. Often confused with Plymouth and other naval ports, Portsmouth is probably best known as the place from whence Admiral Nelson sallied forth in 1805 to beat up the French at the Battle of Trafalgar. Soccer fans may know Pompey as the only team ever to have held the FA Cup for seven years (World War II got in the way), and from some legendary players… and for the notorious 6.57 Crew 'supporters' club.

- Famous sons or sometime residents of the city include engineer Isambard Kingdom Brunel, former Prime Minister James Callaghan, movie star and intellectual Arnold Schwarzenegger and a whole library's-worth of writers from Charles Dickens to Rudyard Kipling, H. G. Wells, Sir Arthur Conan Doyle. And, of course, me.

- 'Pompey' hangs like a glittering jewel or, some might say, snotty dewdrop from the coastline of Hampshire, and is the only island city in the

United Kingdom. A lot of people must like or at least have a reason for living there, as the population density is pretty much the highest in the UK. Portsea Island (which most people think of as Portsmouth) has an area of under twenty-five square miles and a population of more than 200,000. To make a basic comparison, coming up for 150 people occupy every square kilometre in Wales. In Pompey it is a tad over 5000. Yep, that's *five thousand*.

- Despite this enforced cheek-to-jowl neighbourliness, Pomponians can be very welcoming to outsiders, unless they diss our fair city or hail from Southampton.

- Like all naval ports, Pompey has long played host to peoples and ships from around the world. We were multi-cultural before it was trendy, and that must have contributed significantly to the city's character and culture. Then there's how our seagoing history has resulted in Portsmouth having its own accent, and even language. For centuries, young men from inland locations across Britain would be drawn by exotic tales of roving the seven seas to come to Portsmouth and join the Royal Navy. They would then marry a local girl and start a family. Across the centuries, this has enriched the city's range of traditions, attitudes and even vocabulary as you can see at the end of the book.

- Together with its unique island status, Pompey has some interesting firsts and lasts, like for example:

The first-ever UFO sighting in Britain to be recognised and investigated by the Ministry of Defence occurred over Portsmouth in 1950

- Sir Arthur Conan Doyle attended his first séance in Portsmouth and was converted to Spiritualism in 1887, the year the first Sherlock Holmes novel was published

- Arrested in Portsmouth in 1944, Helen Duncan was the last woman in Britain to be charged with Conjuring Spirits under the 1735 Witchcraft Act

- The first dry dock in England was built in Portsmouth in 1497

- Tobacco was first smoked in England on Portsmouth High Street in 1604. Legend has it that a woman thought the sailors having a smoke were on fire and threw the contents of a chamber pot over them.

1961

~ Impresario Berry Gordy signs Diana Ross and her group to the Motown label, with the proviso they change their name from the Primettes to the Supremes

~ John F Kennedy is sworn in as the 35th President of the United States

~ Ham the chimp becomes the first ape in space, being sent 157 miles above the Earth

~ Marilyn Monroe is locked in a padded cell in a Los Angeles psychiatric hospital four days after the release of what will be her last film, *The Misfits*

~ The Beatles make the first of their 292 appearances at the Cavern Club, Liverpool

~ Mattel release the 'Ken' doll, introducing him as Barbie's boyfriend

~ On board the Vostok1, Russian cosmonaut Yuri Gagarin becomes the first human to cross into outer space

~ Found guilty of spying for the Soviet Union, double agent spy George Blake is jailed for 42 years. After five he will escape and flee to Moscow

~ Ballet-dancing sensation Rudolf Nureyev defects from the Soviet Union to France

~ Future Princess of Wales Diana Spencer is born at Sandringham

~ At 61, author Ernest Hemmingway dies from a self-inflicted gunshot wound

~ A car in the Italian Grand Prix hits a barrier, killing the driver and fifteen spectators.
~ Minister of Health Enoch Powell announces that oral contraceptive pills would become available through the NHS
~ Adolf Eichmann is found guilty of crimes against humanity in WWII and sentenced to death

Top Tunes

Number One records for the year included:

I Love You ~ Cliff Richard and the Shadows
Poetry in Motion ~ Johnny Tillotson
Are you Lonesome Tonight? ~ Elvis Presley
Sailor ~ Petula Clark
Walk Right Back ~ Everly Brothers
Blue Moon ~ The Marcels
Runaway ~ Del Shannon
Johnny Remember Me ~ John Leyton
Walkin' Back to Happiness ~ Helen Shapiro
Kon Tiki ~ The Shadows
Running Scared ~ Roy Orbison
Moon River ~ Danny Williams
You're Driving me Crazy ~ The Temperance Seven
Michael (row the boat ashore) ~ The Highwaymen

I'm a walking in the rain
Tears are fallin' and I feel a pain
A wishin' you were here by me
To end this misery
And I wonder, I wa wa wa wa wonder
Why, why, why, why, why, why,
She ran away
And I wonder where she will stay
My little runaway
A run run run run Runaway

Runaway by Del Shannon. Lyrics by Del Shannon
and Max Crook

In truth it was a real crock, but to me the battered old motorbike looked as sleek and full of menace as a crouching panther.

I saw the same model advertised on eBay the other day with an asking price of a shade under £5000. At £32 after haggling, my 1953 MAC Velocette was, in those far-off days and as we old people like to say, still a lot of money. At ten bob a week it would take more than a year to pay Mother back, but the Beast was now all mine.

The vendor was a shifty-looking sailor who said he had to sell his beloved bike as he was off on a long sea voyage and had nowhere to store it. According to him, it had been converted at great expense for use on race tracks, which would account for its strange and, as he said, racy appearance. He also said it should go without saying that it went like the clappers. I had handed over the money and watched him walk off before I was to find it did not go like the clappers, but was certainly clapped out.

Unlike the mass-produced bikes from giant British manufacturers like Norton, Triumph, Vincent and BSA, Velocettes were hand-made by a family firm in Birmingham. They were a small concern, but more than held their own in racing circles and won two world championships in the late Forties and early Fifties. To me and most of my biker mates, Velocette was associated with the maroon coloured, water-cooled 'Noddy bikes' ridden by police patrolmen like our persecutor-to-be, PC Jennings.

My bike had been much tinkered with, and was unlike the standard road model.

In those days, accessories and add-ons were more than scarce. People had to improvise if they wanted to customise their bikes, and mine had certainly been customised. The distinctive Velocette 'fishtail' had been replaced with a megaphone-style exhaust with its spout painted a fiery red. The home-made racing saddle was uncomfortable and had no room for a pillion passenger. Most striking of all were the handlebars. Rather than the norm, there were two short, chromed tubes clamped to the top of the front forks. They certainly looked racy, but the dents either side of the hump-backed tank showed the limit of their movement. They may have been okay for the curves of a racetrack circuit, but not for a ninety degree turn into a side road in an urban setting.

~

There was something else the vendor had not told me. My black beast would not fire-up in the normal way. There was a kick-start, but repeatedly kicking it did not start the engine and just flooded the carburettor. As I discovered, the only way to get the engine to do its job was with what was known as a bump start, which should more properly have been known as a bum start.

I don't know the science behind it, but the trick involved shoving the heavy bike along the road as fast as I could run, then leaping aboard and letting the clutch out as my bottom hit the seat. If it worked, the engine caught and I was off. As well as effective, it looked impressive and some lairy riders would deliberately do a bump-start when they didn't need to. Some daring riders would even jump on side-saddle before standing up, cocking a leg over, settling down and roaring off. My bike was great at the roaring bit, but not at reaching a speed which threatened my quiff. I don't know how powerful the old Velo had been when young, but its racing days were long over when it became mine.

Six decades on, the Eastern Road is still one of the only three highways by which to escape from Portsmouth. These days it can be hard to reach let alone break the speed limit because of traffic lights, other hindrances and volume of traffic. In the Sixties, it was an unofficial racetrack and favoured site for burn-ups. I remember local biking legend 'Nellie' Burns picking me up from home on his new BSA 650 cc Super Rocket. He said he was heading for the Eastern Road to check that it could comfortably exceed a ton (100mph) with two up and needed me to make up the weight. It did, and I burned my feet quite badly on the exhausts as he hadn't given me time to put my shoes or socks on.

Unsurprisingly and despite much less volume of

traffic in those days, the injury and death rate on the Eastern Road was shockingly high, and I was to lose several mates in bike and car crashes.

Although it looked the business, the problem with my aged Velo was that it could not be coaxed above a relatively pedestrian sixty-five miles an hour; and that with a following wind and me lying flat on the petrol tank. In truth this was not a problem, as I was never a real biker with a need for speed. I just liked tooling around Portsmouth, looking cool and dropping to not much more than walking speed when passing a pretty girl. My quiff would stay in place, and the deep, throaty and slow thump of the engine gave no indication of its real limitations. Nobody outside our small circle of mates knew my secret. As one of those scornfully said, my bike was a bit like me. It looked the dog's bollocks, but it was all show and no go. I would have remonstrated, but he was much bigger than me.

~

Apart from its potential as a bird puller, my new old bike cut hours off the daily trip to and from Warsash. Somewhat ironically, the job was nearing completion and I would soon be off to another site somewhere in the South.

I would in some ways be sad to leave, as I had got to know and like my workmates, and even held grudging respect for C**t Dracula. After the early days of pipe painting and lugging sacks of fittings about, running errands and making tea, I was now literally getting to grips with my trade. My main job with a mate would be to get the pipes ready for screwing together. It sounds easy, but cost a lot of hacksaw blades and pipe before I learned the trick. Threading the pipes would be done with an ingenious device called a Presto Threader. The dies would be set to the precise depth of thread needed, and a long handle used to turn the heavy piece of kit. It was hard work, and some of the older labourers clearly felt it. One of the fitter's mates was a Welshman predictably known as Taff or The Goat Shagger. He seemed ancient to me, but was probably in his sixties. After we got to know each other, he told me he was one of only three survivors of the sinking of HMS Hood, a battle cruiser which went down with over 1,400 men in 1941. I don't know if that was true, but there was something about him and his manner that made it seem so. Sometimes, I would see him pause and look thoughtfully as if into the past. Although sometimes in pain with arthritis, he would never complain, and perhaps he felt he should be grateful that he was still alive and not laying with his shipmates on the sea bed. When it was a particularly heavy job, I tried to take the weight off his old shoulders, but could tell he resented it.

~

The final deadline for the heating system to be inspected, tested and officially handed over to the main contractor was close. The pipes had been screwed or welded into place, radiators fitted and the new boiler installed.

As Charlie said, the Big Stink Day would be some-time during the next week. This, he explained was when the heating was turned on to check the system was watertight. The name came about because, despite the piss buckets on every floor, men would often relieve themselves where they stood. The urine would soak into the porous breeze block walls and then be plastered over. When the system was turned on, the heat from the radiators would bring out a ferocious odour, rivalling the smell of the toilet block at Fratton Park.

But before the system could be tested, all work would need to be completed. This, announced our dearly beloved foreman 'Count (or to some, C*nt) Dracula', would mean a ghoster.

This was a not uncommon practice that most workers viewed with a mixture of enthusiasm and trepidation. A ghoster was called for when a deadline loomed and made it necessary to work non-stop through the day, that night and the next day. We started on the morning of the following Thursday, worked till the normal knocking-off time, then took a break before starting again. Next morning, we took an hour to fall asleep over breakfast, then carried on until that evening. Obviously there would be a bit of skiving and even getting heads down while others kept watch, but with Count Dracula in his element after dark and likely to appear at any time, there was little respite. We went home on the Friday tired but happy, with double time at night meaning we had earned almost a week's wages in two days. I would be better off by more than a fiver and would be too knackered that evening to go out and spend it, so it was a double saving.

~

The evenings were getting lighter, and I was enjoying summer seafront posing on the Velo. Thumping slowly and repeatedly up and down alongside the promenade or pulling noisily into the playground of my local youth club, I really felt I was King of the Road. I was not alone in having bought my first bike, and we had the makings of a gang.

We were a mixed bunch, but of an age and mind. There was easy-going Ernie, cleverly sardonic Johnny Nick, two Colins (one of them being Wilkie of the white-topped stage shoes). Little Mac and Big Jim. As a group we had no name or purpose; we just liked each other and our bikes. They loved going on jaunts to London and sitting around in legendary biker caffs like The Ace while talking biker talk. I was very much a fair-weather fan, and really saw my Velo as an additional aid to posing.

~

Nowadays, Harley and Davidson, Honda Electra Glide, Motto Guzzi and other superbikes are almost common. In our day, it was really something to own a powerful, quick bike with a legendary name. You'd see them at coffee shops and transport caffs in Portsmouth where bikers liked to gather and talk of compression ratios and re-bores and the like. One of the most popular gathering places for those enamoured by big, big-name bikes was Bert's Cafe.

Alongside a long, wide and mostly untroubled road on the outskirts of the city, Bert's specialised in fry-ups, bacon sandwiches and doorstep-sized slices of dripping toast. The mugs were man-sized and the tea strong, and Bert's was the in place for local bikers to gather to show off their bikes, tell tall tales and indulge in regular 'burn-ups.' This was when you took on another bike in an urban road race. A particular speciality at Bert's was the round-the-roundabout challenge. This involved the contestant sitting astride his bike with the engine running while someone put a specified record on the juke box. The challenge was for him to race towards the city, past the Smith's Crisps and Johnsons baby powder factory, round the roundabout there and then back to Bert's before the record ended. In those days, most pop songs lasted less than three minutes, so it was rare that the deadline was beaten.

I was half-jestingly challenged once, and to the surprise of the regulars picked up the metaphorical gauntlet. This was not because I fancied risking my neck, but fancied a greasy biker's long-legged and big-breasted pillion passenger. Ever the dramatist, I chose *Tell Laura I Love Her* as my record. The theme of doom-laden Ritchie Valens song was of a love-lorn teenager who dies in a car crash, and had been briefly barred by the BBC for fear it might encourage listeners to commit suicide.

With a soulful look at the curvaceous bikerette, I squared my shoulders, turned up the collar of my jacket and left.

Although I thought about pretending to do the full journey, I decided to have a real go at beating the time challenge. Though limited to sixty-five mph top speed, my bike was no slouch at acceleration. Accordingly, I roared off and took what I thought were near-insane risks overtaking and cutting-up other road users. Back at Bert's, I dropped my bike on its side when I arrived and rushed in to hear the

dying strains of *Tell Laura I Love Her*.

The balloon of my elation was pricked when the referee told me I had taken so long he had put the record on twice.

~

Serious bikers went for leather jackets which could cost more than my old Velo. On my way to work I looked more like Wurzel Gummidge than a Wild One.

In wintertime I'd wear one of my brother's old overcoats, shrouded with a plastic Pac-a-Mac raincoat tied round the middle with string. Instead of knee-high fleece-lined leather boots, it would be wellies with the tops turned down. Helmets did not become compulsory wear until 1973, and many bikers would rather be seen dead than wearing one. Many got their wish, but I had promised my mother I would wear a helmet. To avoid looking like a Nancy boy, I alternated between World War II tin helmets of both British and German varieties.

When cruising around the town in the evenings and weekend, I would choose a denim jacket with the collar turned up, a fashion inspired by the sulky and short-lived film star James Dean. He had died in a car crash some years before, but his legend lived on. He'd sported almost as cool a quiff as me, and with his blonde hair, high cheekbones and snub nose, I could see that we were not unalike.

I suppose I have always had one of those faces that, apart from punching, people liked to see as containing some aspect of any number of movie and pop stars. At that time the list included Glen Ford,

Billy Fury, Cliff Richard and even the darkly handsome Terence Stamp. In later years it would always be actor and serious drinker and brawler Oliver Reed. We had a set-to when we met in a Southsea hotel and he told me he did not like the look of my face and was going to change it. But that's another story.

After taking her to a re-run of *Rebel Without a Cause*, I asked a fleeting girlfriend if she thought I had, like James Dean, a mean and moody look. She thought about it a bit, then, using the Pompey usage of the word, said I was certainly full of moody (bullshit). Going by how often she had to buy the drinks when I claimed to be boracic (broke or skint as in lint), she added, I must be one of the meanest boys she had ever gone out with.

~

Vintage sports cars, the guitar and proper rock 'n' roll music being prime examples, time has not staled some fashionable things of my youth. A new sensation from across the Atlantic were denim jeans.

Girls then would not have believed that their granddaughters would pay a small fortune for jeans which came with ragged holes in them. For young women then, their jeans had to look pristine... and be as tight as nature allowed. To achieve this customised shrink-fit, they would sit in a new pair in a bath of cold water.

We blokes liked to look like Clint Eastwood as Rowdy Yates in *Rawhide*, so needed our denims to look lived-in. Like many, I would soak mine in a bath of cold water with a cupful of bleach added, then put them on the top of the coal bunker in the yard and beat them with half a wall brick until they looked sufficiently worn. The irony was that I wore baggy, oily jeans on the buildings all day, but had to distress new ones to look right when out on the town. They had to be new and squeaky clean, but look well-worn.

Some people used industrial strength bleach to give their new jeans a really faded and well-used look, but that was risky. Mick Beacon overdid it once by emptying a bottle of his mum's drain cleaner into the bath and getting in with his new Lee Coopers on. They disintegrated and he was limping for a week with a very sore crotch.

~

Tommy Steele found fame at the 2i's coffee bar in Soho. My solo career started and finished on the same day at the Expresso Bongo in Arundel Street.

The classiest and oldest dedicated coffee house in Portsmouth was Verrecchia's in the Guildhall Square. People of all ages had long gathered there to drink in the incomparable bouquet of freshly roasted beans and delicious vanilla ice cream. There was the posh Continental Café nearby and the Swiss Café in Edinburgh Road, but elsewhere it was generally caffs or tea rooms.

Then in the early 60's, coffee bars became all the rage as meeting places for youngsters too cool to go to youth clubs and too young to go to pubs.

All around the city, former groceries, haberdasheries and cycle repair shops were being refurbished, kitted out and given exotic names. Some had real Espresso machines for making frothy-topped milky coffee. Those on a tighter budget made up the latte of the day with energetic stirring and making gurgling sounds in the kitchen. Coffee was served in see-through cups and saucers made of the same glass as ovenproof dishes. They were supposed to be unbreakable but that did not always prove to be true, and were the source of many bad jokes involving Pyrex and Durex.

Café society would sit for hours eyeing up the talent across the rim or even through the cup, and I became almost addicted to the drink and the settings. I would do the rounds of the Expresso Bongo, Matador, Beachcombers, Delmonico's and Manhattan... and the even more exotically named Esperanto. They were the places in which to be, to see and be seen and sometimes entertained by local performers like Jon Isherwood and Pat Nelson.

To get in on the act and despite my lack of talent, I summoned up the courage and took my Hoffner Club guitar along to the Milano and laid it casually on the table.

Unfortunately, or perhaps not, there was nowhere to plug the amplifier in and the place was filled with bikers playing rock anthems on the juke box. They and the owners did not take kindly to my request to turn it off, so I mimed a few hits like *Kon-tiki* and *Apache* while doing the Shadow walk and left the actual playing and performing for another day that I knew would never dawn.

~

Despite my world-class quiff, cool clothes and regular attendance at youth clubs, coffee bars and pubs across the city, the only legovers I was getting regularly were across the saddle of my old motor bike.

Whatever people say about the licentious goings-on during the Swinging Sixties, at its start there was still a very traditional (i.e. old-fashioned) and restrictive view of recreational sex. Basically, it was that you shouldn't have any until married. This premier rule for living was particularly drummed into young women and God help her if she fell pregnant and did not immediately get married to the father.

Once again, I need to make it clear I'm neither recommending nor defending the mores and moral stances of the past. I'm just saying how it was, and why we young men were obsessed with getting our end away... or even close to it. Some, like me, were more obsessed than others, but we were, after all, only obeying Mother Nature's instructions.

Unrequited or eternal declarations of love might be the plaintive wail of all those pop singers, but what we really wanted was to get our legs over. In a society where having full-on sex is regarded as no more significant than going for a hamburger, it must be hard to see how frustrating the social norms of the time were for young men, and perhaps, young women. Whatever my male contemporaries might claim, getting your end away was very rare.

It was something to boast about if you even got your hand up a girl's sweater or inside her blouse, and there were other generally agreed levels of success. The first was having a feel over the top of her bra; the next was to get your fingers under it, and I became something of an expert at the sneaky one-handed hook-and-eye fastener quick-release trick. Sometimes it was allowed; at other times it triggered outrage and signalled the end of the snogging session. More than anything, getting your hand above the stocking-top line made your heart boom like an Eric Delaney drum solo, and any further progress was something to really brag about. Some claimants would not wash for days so they could offer evidence of their success. Others faked it, and one outrageous boaster was known to stick his right forefinger into a jar of Shipham's Potted Shrimp Paste so he could regularly claim a stinky finger.

One of the boys at Eastney Youth Club had a matchbox containing a single tightly curly black hair he said had become lodged in his underpants during an encounter with a woman known locally as Freda the Forces' Favourite. The general consensus was that it might have been one of hers, but without inarguable provenance it could equally have been one of his own.

Since my initiation ceremony with *Humps 'n' Bumps Hilda, my excursions beyond the pantie line could be counted on the fingers of one hand, so to speak, and my legovers on the fingers of no hands.

Then I met Mandy, and she took me to repressed teenage male heaven.

Curiously and like my primary school fiancé and my fantasy lover Jilly, Mandy had what was known then as a lazy eye, or unkind people would call a squint. Don't ask me why, but I obviously found that slightly out-of-focus look very sexy.

Apart from the occasionally wandering eye, Mandy

was tall for the times and had firm strong features and a delicate retroussé nose, framed by shoulder-length, ash-blonde hair. She favoured (as did I) the fashionable combination of blouse and pencil skirt, separated by a wide belt. She had milky, almost translucent skin, and underneath the blouse were very large and very white dough-like breasts, kept almost in order by a brassiere I reckoned to be a couple of sizes too small. This was not to be provocative, she told me, but because they didn't make them in her cup size unless as part of an armoured ensemble favoured by older ladies.

We met at a youth club, and it took only two attempts before I was allowed access to all areas. Mandy was quiet, undemanding, and I think, loved me, which made the end of our affair even worse.

Because she was so available and undemanding, I treated her badly, and would summon her after band rehearsals or a trip to the pub for a visit to the Humps 'n' Bumps. As dusk fell, she would, according to my whim, strip slowly or quickly down to her stockings and I would sate myself as she lay back on or bent over a slab of concrete or an abandoned sofa.

Our relationship ended with the summer, when she said she did not want to see me again. Unable to believe she could free herself of my charms, I demanded an explanation. Crying, she said that she had been approached at Eastney youth club by a trio of my biker friends. They had asked her to go with them to the seafront for a group session. When she had refused and asked why they thought she would do that, they had said that I had told them how easy she was, and what we got up to at the

Humps 'n' Bumps.

When she asked if what they had said was true, I could not deny it, and that was the last I saw of my Mandy. It should have taught me a lesson, but I fear it did not.

As detailed in Pompey Lad - Part One, the Humps 'n' Bumps was a local name for an area of wasteland near Hayling Ferry, used for fly-tipping, sexual liaisons and general getting-up-to-no-good.

At work I was beginning to feel at ease amongst the black humour, rough conviviality and eternal banter. Cruel tricks like stealing or defiling sandwiches or setting booby traps were the norm, and anything but a serious accident was greeted with ribald remarks and laughter.

I particularly remember a tall labourer forgetting to duck and knocking himself out on a horizontal scaffold pole. Rather than rush to his aid, there were howls of laughter and the piss-taking went on for days. Perhaps it was how men had learned to rub along amongst the dirt and danger, but that's how it was then. I suspect it would have been little different on a ship of the line in Nelson's navy.

As a fairly green apprentice boy, I was more or less on a level with a labourer in the hierarchy, and on call to work with any of the fitters when an extra pair of hands was needed. From them I learned something about the trade, and a lot about men who were old enough to have seen action in the War.

Colin and Robbie Pratt were the sons of the big, bluff manager who had delivered me to the site on my first day. Like many brothers, they were poles

On the job: Health & Safety rules were not at the top of the agenda.

apart in some aspects of their character and attitude. Robbie was a big, bear-like man with an acerbic wit. When I dropped a heavy fitting on my foot or broke yet another hacksaw blade, he would look steadily at me, roll his eyes, shake his head and cross himself. He was single and, to the envy of most of the married men, lodged in a Southsea pub. It was of course said that he helped the landlady out when her husband was not on the premises.

Colin Pratt was as tall as his brother and as thin as Robbie was rotund. I think this may have been because he was as mean with feeding himself as every other aspect of his life. Where his brother and the other fitters would wear heavy boots, Colin wore plimsolls. I remember him turning up on an icy winter day in plimsolls and a brightly coloured, short-sleeved beach shirt he said he had bought at a knock-down price at Woolworths. For me, his saving grace was his slow smile and sharp sense of humour. He knew who and what he was and what other people thought of him, and just didn't care.

As short as the brothers Pratt were tall, Neville Ray reminded me of a blond Norman Wisdom. One of twins, he was an accomplished and enthusiastic ballroom dancer, and a genuinely funny man. A career as a redcoat at Butlins would probably have suited him better than joining pipes together. My particular memory of him is his ready smile and quip, and how he tried to teach me to waltz. It must have been a bizarre sight as two men in overalls and toe-tector boots shuffled around the gas bottles, the smaller one taking the lady's part as, he said, it was harder to do the steps backwards while remembering to keep your chin up and a smile on your face.

What with Count Dracula the foreman, Old Taff, Ginger Charlie and Neville the dancing instructor, my colleagues could have been seen as an odd bunch. To me, they were just ordinary men who had grown up in hard times and learned in their own ways how to get on with life.

~

Nowadays and thanks to TV exposure and the creation of multi-millionaire superhero players, snooker halls can be quite cool places. Not so in the early Sixties when they were dark, dingy and often dangerous places.

The North End Snooker Club was to be found at the end of a narrow alley off London Road. A busy greengrocer's shop fronted the road, and the alleyway was used to dump crater's, cartons and mounds of dying and dead fruit and veg. Beyond them, the black-painted steel-plate-reinforced double -doors of the club gave the false impression that there were things of value inside.

Beyond the doors and away from the light of day, the North End Snooker Club was pretty much a blueprint for every other place of its kind in the city, and probably the country.

The interior was as dark as a tomb, the only illumination coming from the shaded lights above the half-dozen sadly distressed tables and a single bulb above the alcove where tables were hired and refreshments ordered and served. A thick fug of cigarette smoke hung suspended in the table lights, curiously even when there were no customers on the premises. More smoke issued from the pot-bellied stove beside the alcove and upon which sat an outsized tin kettle. In pride of place stood a Jennings mechanical fruit machine, with a carved Red Indian head above the glass fronted pay-out box. On the nearby counter, a murky glass cabinet imprisoned rather than displayed the infamous meat pies which were said to have a life of their own. Itwas a favourite Christmas story of my father's that they came with the club, and the first customer to buy one had complained that the inside was green. With a fairly straight face, my dad had told him it was a new idea he was testing out and included steamed spinach with the prime beef. The same customer bought it in both senses, then complained that his next pie was spinachless, and demanded a refund or discount.

It was my first visit to the new family business, and my father introduced me with a suitably proprietorial manner. He seemed thoroughly at home, and comfortable in his bulky cardigan, droopy flannels and slippers, the roll-up hanging from his mouth adding to the miasma.

Before I attended to the reason for my visit, dad introduced me to his staff. Charlie was a diminutive man with a thyroid condition probably not helped by the lack of daylight and the haze of smoke. He wore his hair in a combover, and had obviously left his teeth at home.

Then I met the regulars, who, in the way of those times, all had names not given them at birth. There were two Wackers, a Banjo, a Black Man (who was of course very blond) a Tosher, a Bees and a Tonto. A rough-looking lot, they seemed amiable enough, and my Glaswegian giant dad was big and experienced enough to keep them in order.

I was at the club to use my newly-learned skills to fit a new pipe to the bottom of the tin trough that acted as a urinal. Someone had stolen the original copper u-bend and piping for its scrap value during the hand-over process, and nobody had noticed till someone had got really wet feet. Within an hour I had installed a heavy metal pipe running from the urinal to a hole in the yard. The pipe would not be worth stealing, and I had not looked too closely at the hole into which it delivered its golden showers. Work done, my dad suggested a drink in the social club which sat above his little empire.

At the top of a flight of concrete steps which would have been no fun falling down, the long room with a bar and some Formica-topped tables had a name far more exotic than its homely setting. This was quite usual.

Like many such places in the city, The Oasis was a watering hole with a benign view of membership, house rules and the restrictions of licensing hours. The club, my dad explained, was most popular on Sunday lunchtimes when there was a meat raffle, and any evening after the pubs chucked out. Dad added that the police occasionally stopped by for refreshment, and potential troublemakers were warned to behave by a poster on the wall. It showed a man, helpless in a neck lock administered by a ferocious looking, bearded giant. Big Bruno Elrington was a former Royal Marine and now professional wrestler, whose wife ran a poodle parlour. He was even taller than my dad, and a gentleman in the proper sense of the word. As my father said, the cautionary poster was surprisingly effective even when Bruno was not on duty as part-time bouncer.

We had another drink, and my father told me he knew the snooker club was a pretty tatty place, but the fruit machine took more than the table hire, and was all profit. Giant oaks from small acorns grew, and one day he would own the biggest and best and most respectable snooker club in the South.

He was right, and in years to come all the major snooker stars would come to show off their skills at the Craneswater Club. My favourite was the erratic and contrary genius Alex 'Hurricane' Higgins, who I served two dozen Bloody Marys before watching him effortlessly destroy the best players in the club while making more than a dozen hundred breaks. I would have liked to have got to know him better and he was to have stayed at our home overnight as part of his fee. Sadly, he decided to set his car on fire and kick me in the balls before running off into the night, but that, like my meeting with Ollie Reed, is another story for another time.

~

Our work done at Warsash, the team had been split up and sent to other sites in and around Portsmouth. I had been posted to a defunct aerodrome on a hill on the road between Portsmouth and Southampton.

Twenty years before, the giant hangars had been home to anti-aircraft blimps. Now the site was to be made ready for the National Census. The survey and registration of every person in the land took place each decade, and the buildings had to be updated to accommodate the workers.

For me, it was not a good move for two reasons. After a shaky start, at Warsash I had begun to learn my trade and been encouraged to use the tools of the trade. Here I was to spend several months doing repetitive no-brainer manual work, and all the while exposed to a material now recognised as a stone-cold killer.

My first close encounter with asbestos came when I was told to take a pair of tin snips, a hammer and oxy-acetylene cutting torch to the miles of above-ground heating pipes connecting the old accommodation huts.

The pipes sat on brick tiers, and were insulated with a thick, hand-moulded coating of asbestos wrapped in roofing felt which was held in place with chicken wire. This had to be removed before the pipes could be cut up and removed, and the advised approach was to cut through the chicken wire, unwrap the felt, and then attack the asbestos lagging with a lump hammer.

The lagging exploded when struck, and though it was in the open air, I still finished the day looking like a ghost.

The situation was even more deadly in the boiler room. When the old boiler and pipes had been replaced, the laggers would arrive. Their job was to knock up vats of what looked like porridge and then mould the stuff on to the pipes. It was fascinating to watch them in action, but not a healthy place to be. The process would begin with the emptying of sacksful of asbestos flakes into a tall metal drum, the adding of water, then the stirring of the mix with a paddle the size and shape of a dinghy oar. When the powdered asbestos was being poured into the drum, the boiler house would look like one of those glass balls you shake to create a winter wonderland scene. It was hard to see through the miasma of potentially deadly particles, let alone avoid inhaling them. In those rudimentary health and safety days, there was provision of a daily pint of milk when the laggers were on the job so as to, as the foreman said, keep the dust down.

Nowadays we know what a killer asbestos is. All the laggers I knew are dead, and most died well before their time. I've been amazingly lucky, so far.

~

Perhaps it was my disenchantment with my job or the lack of success with the band and putting my willy where I felt it belonged, but my life was becoming increasingly punctuated by acts of violence. Often initiated by me, but sometimes I was just the victim.

This was why one Monday morning I found myself sitting in a dentist's waiting room, feeling particularly sorry for myself.

I'd been given a kicking, lost a chunk of a front tooth and been thrown through the window of an off-licence. To make things worse, I had to pay for the window, and even worse I was innocent of the reason I was thrown through it.

I'd expected just another evening when I tarted myself up, put on my Italian box jacket suit, and visited a youth club in Albert Road. I was still spending more time in youth clubs than pubs; not because I couldn't get in, but you had more chance of pulling a bird in a youth club than in most pubs. To summon up the nerve to smooth-talk a suitable victim, I would take a couple of pints on board before arriving. On this occasion, I had downed at least one too many rough ciders.

I certainly felt no pain when I was set on by three youths who I was on nodding terms with. It started with a head butt and then a rain of punches before I went through the window of an off-licence. Next door to the shop was a coffee bar run by a tough middle-aged guy called Jim. He arrived, broke the one-sided fight up, staunched the flow of my blood with a tea-towel and asked what the scrap had been about.

The regular girl friend of the main protagonist was a pretty little blonde girl, and he said I had been seen chatting her up. When he had approached me in the street, I had attacked him and his mates and they had done no more than defend themselves. I honestly could not remember talking to his girlfriend or setting about the trio, but looking for trouble after a few pints was to become a bit of a trademark for me in coming years.

~

This was getting silly. For the second time in a month, I had been attacked in the street by superior forces.

On this occasion I'd been innocently standing by the milk machine in Milton Road after a game of darts in my local when a Triumph 500 screeched to a stop on the other side of the road. The rider and passenger dismounted, and I assumed they had stopped for a carton of strawberry-flavoured milk. In fact, they had stopped to give me a kicking.

The rider had taken his helmet off and swung it at me before I had a chance to drop my drink and defend myself. Despite how they depict it in cartoons, it's not true you see stars when you get a heavy blow to the head, but I certainly saw some flashing lights. As I went down, the pillion passenger kicked me in the stomach, and through the pain I noted how almost balletically it was done.

As I sensibly stayed down and lay there with arms over my head, the rider used his steel toe-capped knee-length biker boots to give me another one to the guts.

Before they left, he picked up my carton of milk and poured what was left in it over my new, four-button pin stripe Italian Jacket. As I watched them through a rapidly closing eye, I saw how differently the pillion passenger walked from the rider. The buttocks in the tight blue jeans were swaying with each step and I realised I'd been kicked while down by a female.

The next day I took my new jacket into the cleaners, and when I told the boys about the incident I didn't mention that one of my assailants was of the opposite sex. When I wondered why they had attacked me, the general view was that I had committed some offence against them, but little Mac pointed out that even at a distance and doing nothing, I looked really lairy.

~

In my childhood, gents' hairdressers offered little more than a short-back-and-sides for men, and a basin cut for boys. Other services included placing an illegal off-course bet, or something for the weekend in the shape of a small brown envelope. Ladies had their salons, but many did their own washing, colouring and perming at home.

Then, as with coffee bars and Green Shield stamps, posh women's salons and beauty parlours seemed to sprout everywhere, and men started taking an interest in having their hair styled as well as cut. Once only displaying a range of Brylcreem jars and perhaps a jar of dead flowers, the windows of former barber's shops would boast life-sized photographs of smiling young men with improbably crimped and waved hair. I never saw anyone wearing one in real life, but I think they were free window dressing and a statement of intent.

If you lived in my part of the city or even beyond, a regular Saturday visit would be to famed tonsorialist Al Moody's. His establishment was the only male hairdresser I can remember where queues formed before opening time.

He was a sturdy and affable man, and practised his art in Highland Road opposite the caff above which my mother was born. He was always cheerful despite how his feet must have ached after a long Saturday session, and he told the filthiest jokes of any barber I ever knew.

The prevailing odour inside the salon every Saturday was a blend of Friday night farts, nicotine, setting lotion, bay rum, Brylcreem and singed hair. I suppose some customers called in for a standard trim, but I never saw anyone in the chair under thirty who did not ask for a blow job.

The thing about Al was he played by his rules. There was a limited choice of cuts and styles on offer, and when you had chosen one, your job was to sit and submit. I never saw him refuse to give a man a style he did not think would suit him, but you had the feeling he would.

Most popular in those days was the Elvis/Cliff quiff with variations. Any blow wave would be set rigid with a hairdryer which could have stripped wallpaper. Al would always ask if it was too hot, but I never knew a customer to say yes. It would have been a Nancy Boy thing to do in front of your peers, and was a demonstration of hardness to sit apparently relaxed but with your knuckles white on the chair arms under the sheet as your hair was frazzled to the texture of Weetabix.

A curious newcomer in the early Sixties was called a semi-crew. Inspired by American war movies featuring battles at sea, close-cropped 'crew cuts' had become popular in the Fifties. A new twist was to leave a privet hedge-like line of hair at the front which was folded into a frontal quiff over the stubble on top of the head.

Before the style went out of fashion, Teddy Boys would favour a tight double quiff above long wings of hair on each side, swept back to meet at the back and form what was known as a DA or Duck's Arse. It was, if you had seen the style and a duck's arse, a very apt nickname.

Whatever the style, Boston neck shaves were universally popular. This was where, rather than a gradual tapering at the back of the neck, a razor would be used to form a straight line parallel with the collar. If you, like me had a spotty neck, it would be a Low Boston if you wanted to get past the bouncers at the entrance to the Savoy (see later), you would need a High Boston.

The final act in the ritual would be The Singe. Like an acolyte in church, Al Moody would light and pass a wax-covered taper across the finished creation, burning any loose ends. This piece of pure theatre was based on the 19th century belief that each strand of hair contained a fluid and needed sealing off lest it leak away. Al probably knew this was bollocks, but also that it heightened the drama and made the customer feel he was getting his money's worth - and also suffering in the pursuit of the perfect haircut.

~

The year drew on and my disenchantment with pipe strangling grew. I was increasingly dwelling on how right my mother and Mr Vine the Careers Master had been, and how wrong I had been. I was earning good money, but putting threads on the end of pipes and screwing them together was not exactly a challenging or rewarding way to spend a long day. I had also thought working in the open air would suit me, but had forgotten that, despite all the pop songs, summertimes were not eternally sunny, even when you were in love.

I got some relief from the mud and cold and rain when I and other apprentices attended the Technical College in Southampton. Here, we would learn the theory and practice of welding and to this day I can tell you all you will ever need to know about Henry Bessemer and how, in 1856, he developed the first effective method of producing steel with his Converter Method. I'm probably also one of a select crowd who can show you how to wipe a lead joint with a blowtorch and moleskin cloth. A useless skill even then, but someone must have forgotten to take it off the syllabus.

Perhaps predictably, I managed to start the six-week course with a bang.

On my first day, a tall, skinny guy swaggered into the classroom enveloped in the full monte of leather trousers, jacket and 'bone-dome' futuristic helmet. I had heard and seen him arrive and he had deliberately parked his gleaming and very quick Gold Star Clubman next to my old Velo. Through the window, I thought or imagined I saw him looking at it contemptuously as he peeled off his gloves and strode into the building.

Words were exchanged, and desks and chairs tumbled as we rolled around the floor. I lost the bout and suffered a dislocated finger after punching his helmet, but we became friends. Like boxing, it was surprising how many punch-ups ended up with the contestants on good terms. That was not a universal rule, of course.

Our first paid gig. Note the sit-up-and-beg radio 'amplifier' for the tank commander microphone

Christmas was coming, and with it the excitement of performing our first paid gig. The venue was the Pure Drop pub in Buckland, and the occasion was the pay-out on the Christmas Club. The customers would be given their savings and celebrate with a knees-up, and we were top of the bill above a magician and a spoons player.

We spent the week before the event practising furiously, and as manager, roadie and pretend rhythm guitarist, it was my job to sort out the running order and make sure all the kit was in working order. When I dropped in to check all was well with the landlord, I was horrified when he asked if it would be alright to use our microphone to call out the winning numbers for the meat raffle.

With only days to go, I looked at the price of a proper microphone, then went to Ben Grubb's the leading ex-WD supplier in the City, where I picked up a tank commander's microphone for next to nothing. It was made of black Bakelite and had a wire hanging from the bottom, but looked a bit like the real thing.

For a loudspeaker I bought an ancient radio from a junk shop in Highland Road and painted it with some electric-blue gloss left over from dad's sign-writing at Kay's Stores. Then I made a plywood sign bearing the legend *The Dynamic Hot Rods* and glued it over the tuning dial of the old set. We tested it with the tank commander's microphone plugged into the back, and with his mouth pressed to the loudspeaker, I could just about hear Bobby Harrigan's voice coming through it. As I promised him, we would try to persuade Johnny to use brushes instead of drum sticks, and choose numbers which required the vocals to be shouted rather than sung.

~

Personally, I felt our debut went fairly well and that we earned our fee of ten bob and a pint of shandy each.

It was a full house because of the pay-out, and we gave our best in the Snug Bar. It was a shame that most of the customers were the age of our parents, and I noticed that, rather than stay and enjoy the music, they virtually all drank up and left after getting their pay-out.

Towards the end of the evening, a big man with a

bushy moustache and the sort of Crombie overcoat which found favour with London gangsters arrived and bellied-up to the bar. After we finished a *Whole Lotta Shaking*, thanked the non-existent audience and started packing up, he came over and introduced himself as the landlord of the Bridge Tavern, the pub just across the road.

When he asked how much we were getting paid and thinking he was going to offer us a gig, I said I would drop in next day and talk about our terms.

With a broad smile, he twirled his moustache and said he was not after booking us for a gig at his pub. Because of us, he had been swamped by customers escaping from our music. He had come to check out our rates so he could pay us to put on another show at his rival pub and boost his takings.

1962

~ BBC Television broadcasts the first episode of *Z Cars*

~ *Dr No*, the first James Bond movie, starring Sean Connery, is released

~ Britain's first legal casino opens at Brighton

~ Bob Dylan releases his first album

~ Marvel comics releases the first adventures of The Incredible Hulk

~ Pope John XXIII excommunicates Cuba's Fidel Castro

~ Operation Chopper, the first combat mission in the war in Vietnam takes place

~ Three men become the first convicts to escape from Alcatraz prison

~ Algeria wins Independence from France

~ The Rolling Stones perform their first gig at the Marquee Club, London

~ The Beatles perform their first live gig in the UK, and John Lennon marries Cynthia Powell

~ The Beatles release their first single, *Love Me Do*

~ Nelson Mandela is jailed in South Africa

~ An assassination attempt is made on General De Gaulle

~ The Cuban Missile Crisis ends

~ Marilyn Monroe is found dead at her Los Angeles home

My Top Tunes

Rhythm of the Rain ~ The Cascades
Take Good Care of My Baby ~ Bobby Vee
Midnight in Moscow ~ Kenny Ball and his Jazzmen
Stranger on the Shore ~ Mr Acker Bilk
Don'cha Think It's Time ~ Mike Berry and the Outlaws
Let there be Drums ~ Sandy Nelson
Happy Birthday Sweet Sixteen ~ Neil Sedaka
I'll Never Find Another You ~ Billy Fury
Let's Twist Again ~ Chubby Checker
Wimoweh ~ Karl Denver
Dream Baby ~ Roy Orbison
The Hole in the Ground ~ Bernard Cribbins
Sun Arise ~ Rolf Harris
Return to Sender ~ Elvis Presley
Bobby's Girl ~ Susan Maughan
Lovesick Blues ~ Frank Ifield
Bachelor Boy ~ Cliff Richard
The Swiss Maid ~ Del Shannon
Rocking Around the Christmas Tree ~ Brenda Lee

Listen to the rhythm of the falling rain
Telling me just what a fool I've been
I wish that it would go and let me cry in vain
And let me be alone again
The only girl I care about has gone away
Looking for a brand-new start
But little does she know that when she left that day
Along with her she took my heart

Rhythm of the Rain by the Cascades. Lyrics by
John Claude Gummoe

As well as for me, 1962 was to be a significant year for the world, which had been holding its breath since the start of the Cuban Missile Crisis. When Russian leader Nikita Khrushchev backed off, we gave a collective gasp of relief and truly felt we had been on the verge of nuclear holocaust. In my small world, the year would involve a break for freedom from pipe-strangling, another rung on the ladder to pop stardom, learning to fight within the Queensbury Rules, meeting my first true love…and spending my first night in police custody.

~

I started the new year on a new site, but found little change except for where it was. Every building site was the same building site, with the same mud and same cold and wet in winter, and the same sort of people and the same pipes to lug around and fit together all year round.

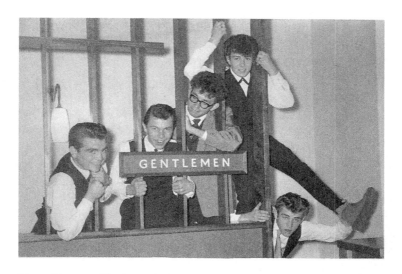

*New Faces: Early publicity shots of the Rockin' Hot Rods with (above) left to right:
Me, Jimbo Lawrence, Sean Conlan, Tony Nabarro and Ricky Cripps.*

I think the numbing boredom of my apprenticeship and fear for a future of being bored and getting dirty for a living was the spur to try and make 1962 the year the Hot Rods made it big.

Probably thanks to my intemperance and our lack of success, we'd regularly lost members since the old washboard and acapella days of the Rhythmic Three. This time it was to be a completely new line-up. Except, of course, for me, who had a knack for finding and training new talent, but not a scrap of that commodity myself.

To go with the new band, I felt it was time for a tweak to our name. Having found that few of our potential fans knew what 'Dynamic' meant, I'd held several meetings with myself and ruled that we would now be known as the Rockin' Hot Rods. Now all I had to do was get the new band to play and co-exist in harmony.

~

With Johnny Witt having moved on, our new drummer was Jim Lawrence. I found him very likeable, highly intelligent and witty in a sometimes-waspish way. In a modern-day boy band, he would have been the Moody One.

Colin Wilkinson had taken his Ricky Nelson pose and white-topped shoes to greater things, and I had found Ricky Cripps, a local boy from an old Milton/Pompey family. In any boy band, Ricky would have been the Good-Looking Quiet One. Another bonus was that he had a proper, four string bass guitar – and one which he knew how to play.

Colin Quaintance and his Fender Stratocaster having

been seduced by a trending local band with the promise of a red stage jacket and a tour of the west country in a proper van, we had a new lead guitarist.

Tony Nabarro was a small, almost baby-faced young man who played a mean guitar and an even meaner harmonica. He was almost impossibly good-looking: think a pocket-sized Tony Curtis at his best. In a boy band, he would have been the Lovable, Great-Looking Cheeky-Faced One. Like Jimmy Lawrence and our new singer, he was a devotee of Blues, and also like our new singer, an enthusiast for experimenting with interesting substances both on and off stage.

My great mate Bobby Harrigan and sole survivor from the early days had moved to live and work in the Channel Isles, and Sean Conlan would be his replacement. Apart from height, the two could not have been much more different. Sean was large-featured and heavily bespectacled, with his thick, woolly black hair exploding into an early version of an Afro-cut. He had a big, powerful voice to match his frame and, like Jimbo Lawrence and Tony Nabbers, had a predilection for ancient and modern Blues. He was also a talented artist and cartoonist, and a bonus was that he came with his own microphone and loudspeaker. He was a lot deeper than he liked to appear, and was even keener on exotic substances than his fellow bandmates. In our imaginary boy band, he would have been the Wacky One.

That left me, the sort of Bruce Welch of the line-up. Unlike the Shadows rhythm guitarist, I was still stuck with my three chords and tin ear. If I had managed to get into any boy band, I suppose I would have been dubbed as The Lairy Surplus One.

~

Though hoping the new group would be my passport to fame and fortune, I was now even more concerned about my lack of musical ability. It would be a bitter blow if, like the Beatles' drummer, I was dumped when the Rockin' Hot Rods made their big breakthrough.

Then it occurred to me that though I couldn't sing or play an instrument, I could ride to success on the back of someone else's music.

I was a big fan of Radio Luxembourg disc jockeys Emperor Rosco, Stuart Henry and Johnny Walker, and would practise my patter by dipping the volume on my transistor radio and talking over their introductions to the hits of the moment. Though crap with any form of music-making, I seemed, as Granny Kelly would say, to have the gift of the gab, and I reckoned that if the band went tits up or I was chucked out, I might be able to make a name for myself as a disc jockey.

I'd already worked out what that name should be, and predictably it was King George. As it transpired, my on-the-road performances were not a success, and I had no idea that in a decade or so I would be hosting rock 'n' roll programmes on and helping run Portsmouth's first local radio station. Unlike managing bands, I seemed to do well shaping Radio Victory, if you don't count it being the first-ever local commercial radio station to lose its license. But, also again, that's another story.

For now, and without any kit except my tranny radio, I was learning the trade at local youth clubs. I'd arrive with an armful of my favourite records and take over the gramophone. If there was a microphone, I'd do my DJ bit...which even then I thought was sometimes bum-clenchingly awful in its banality. Kenny Everett was an inventive genius; I, like Smashy and Nicey, was just a copycat, churning out the predictable cliches in a phoney mid-Atlantic shout. The members at the clubs I imposed my act on did not always take kindly to my tastes, and one evening it got physical.

I was strutting my stuff at St Margaret's Youth Club in Highland Road, playing Hard Hearted Hannah by the Temperance Seven when a big, tough-looking young man came up to the stage and beckoned me over. I bent down and asked him if he had a request, and he said words to the effect of: 'Yeah, stop playing that fucking crap and put something good on'.

One thing led to another, and it being a church hall and deserving of respect, I invited him outside to continue the discussion. Following him towards the door and looking at how really big he was, it occurred to me that I was out of my depth. For the first time and to my shame, I took the coward's way and got the first blow in by hitting him from behind.

Within seconds I was grabbed, thrown across the foyer and slammed up against a wall. I found myself face-to-face with a young black man, who smiled engagingly as he drew his fist back. As if this was not bad enough, I looked over his shoulder and my bowels moved. Looking on and also smiling was the younger brother of the famed and feared Pompey

Ted, Hughie Finnegan. I had obviously just thumped one of his gang.

I shut my eyes and awaited retribution, but the punch never came.

Later and when we became close friends, Patrick Finnegan told me that the reason he and Don Price were smiling was because I looked so terrified, and it seemed a shame to punch somebody so obviously shitting himself...or nearly shitting himself. At the time, as he reminded me, I had gabbled out my apologies and said how I was a fan of his brother, then let out a massive fart of fear.

As I have said before, it was strange how we often met and made friends in those days.

~

We were in the grip of a particularly cruel winter, and I was becoming ever more disenchanted with my chosen career. Now and then I would hear from schoolmates who were learning to be teachers, accountants and solicitors and even one who was studying soil mechanics in Mexico. I would feel like crying when I realised what a mug I'd been, and the irony and even bad joke was that I had got exactly what I'd wanted by leaving school early. I had money in my pocket, a motor bike and plenty of smart clothes, but now saw all too clearly that getting a job with a future and waiting for the accessories would have been a much smarter move.

Apart from the banality of the work, a major reason for my discomfiture was that a building site in winter is a very different place from the summer months.

When the sun shone, I was at times almost content to be young and fit and at work in the open air, building up muscles and getting a tan for free.

When winter arrived, people in offices turned up the heating that people like me had installed, and looked out of the window at the snow and rain. In the lead-up to what became known as The Big Freeze and the hardest winter for two hundred years, we had to use a blowtorch to free a pipe from the frozen pile. When we did break it loose, the icy metal clung to your hands and tore the flesh off your fingertips. Over the course of eight hours, the cold seemed to get through to the very marrow of your bones, and I can't imagine what a heavy day in these conditions must have been like for the older men.

It did not help that my latest posting was to a new office block on the edge of a quay in Southampton Docks.

In the style of the time, the block was being built pagoda-style. That meant it started life with the floors kept apart by no more than concrete pillars, and the external walls of pre-fabricated aluminium and glass being left to last. That meant the wind came roaring in off the Solent and through the half-made building like a really angry banshee. It was so cold that I would get off my bike and start work without removing an item from the five layers of clothing from pack-a-mac to vest. It didn't help that my job was to help with the installation of the giant water tanks that would feed the heating system, and they were located at the very top of the five-storey building.

Every morning as my mother chased me down the

passageway with a ladies' muffler and extra bowl of Ready-Brek to help keep the cold out, I regretted my decision to ignore her wishes and Mr Vine the Careers master's advice. Perhaps it was this that made me so angry and got me involved in so many fights.

Or perhaps my Glaswegian Granny Kelly was right and I just liked a good scrap.

Happy Days: White House Boys and Girls
(Thanks to Big Ernie Sexton and other contributors)

Cover shot: Standing (l to r) Dave 'Budgie' Barron, Johnny 'Smudger' Smith, Les Vear, Johnnie Parkinson, Pat Finnegan and Micky Wicks. Seated: Your author and Charlie 'Dobbo' Dobson

A new set of mates, and a new place to meet them.

In what was to become a pattern, I had moved on from one group of friends to another, and my life began to revolve around pubs, drinking, chasing crumpet and fighting.

Since my escape from retribution at St Margaret's church hall, I'd started to hang around with Pat Finnegan, Don Price and their particular mates Ray Wheatcroft, Jackie Grant and Mickey Wicks.

Inevitably we were to become known as The Finnegan Gang.

Along with a number of similarly-minded young people, our local was the White House in Milton. We would travel around other pubs in the area, but Wilkie's was our HQ.

Before the War, there were more than a thousand corner pubs, taverns, ale-house and gin palaces in Portsmouth. With no telly and sometimes no heat at home, a pub was somewhere you went to nurse a drink and keep warm, socialise, celebrate special occasions, or just get drunk. Thanks to the Luftwaffe, re-development and the shrinking of the Royal Navy, hundreds of Pompey pubs had disappeared. But every area of Portsmouth still had more than its fair share, and because of Fratton Park and the Royal Marine barracks, Milton and Eastney had more than most.

The White House was an unremarkable-looking hostelry, flat-fronted and plain, with none of the over-the-top features of the Brickwood 'folly' pubs. The front elevation was unsurprisingly painted to suit its name. It's now a small terrace of equally unremarkable town houses, and doesn't look as if it was ever a busy boozer. What happened within its walls still stays in my memory, and when passing, I sometimes wonder that there is not even the tiniest echo of its past life left. It seems wrong that all that is dead and forgotten, and I think how fitting it would be if the residents might occasionally hear a ghostly bell clanging for last orders, or smell the fug of stale cigarette smoke and beer and hear the echoes of laughter and singing and a fragment of *At the Hop* on the juke box as they open their front doors.

~

This was to be the decade of great social change, but in the early Sixties, pubs were much of a muchness. Lino on the floor of the Public Bar and carpet in the Lounge or Saloon. The off-licence or Bottle and Jug was where you picked up a packet of crisps, a bottled beer or even a couple of pints in a bath jug. In the Public there might be a shove-ha'penny board and bar billiard table to go with the darts board, but juke boxes or any sort of musical background were rare in the more traditional corner locals. All ale was 'real', and lager beer had yet to take over the counter-tops. Apart from the odd pub offering scrumpy cider, the choice on tap was limited to Mild or Bitter. Bottled beers would include Light and Brown Ale or the stronger barley wine, and ladies could enjoy a half-pint glass of shandy or, lately, a Babycham. Spirits were generally for Christmas or special occasions, as were port and lemons and something yellow and sticky called an Egg Flip.

Catering was mostly limited to crisps, jars of pickled onions and eggs and the odd meat pie or

Scotch Egg. The lack of gastro-pub catering in Portsmouth would be noticeable for another twenty years.

We took our first Pompey pub in 1983, and when I asked the outgoing landlord about catering arrangements, he said they did a few sausage rolls and pies, but them little round things with cheese on top were getting popular. He was I later realised, referring to pizzas.

~

Long before the days of same-sex or single men or women licensees, pubs were run by couples called Dot and Harold or Stan and Vi. Our hosts at the White House were 'Wilkie' Wilkinson (nobody knew his first name) and Greta. Greta liked to fraternise with the customers in the Lounge Bar and on occasion looked in to see we were behaving ourselves, but we never ventured beyond the Public Bar. This was not because we were barred from the Lounge, but because drinks were a penny or more dearer and served in dimpled mugs with handles rather than proper sleeve glasses. With carpet on the floor and toilet paper in the bogs, it was altogether too genteel an atmosphere for us. Also, and Wilkie being a canny landlord, the barmaids in the Lounge were generally older, comfortable women who reminded us of our mums. The girls behind the bar in the Public were younger, prettier and sometimes with unusually big tits.

As for house rules, our hosts were generally more than tolerant and anything short of a bloody punch-up or vomiting over an innocent customer would be tolerated. Wilkie and Greta knew that we youngsters had money and liked to spend it, and our presence would keep foreign troublemakers out.

Having been in the trade for many years, the couple were no longer young and Wilkie spent much of his time upstairs. Like all landlords, rumours about him were many, and it was even said he had new-fangled movie cameras fixed above the tills so he could make sure the barmaids were not cheating him. It was also said he liked using the zoom control to look down the front of their dresses.

~

At work I found myself increasingly resentful of having to get up in the dark, put on smelly, stained clothes and face a day of dirt and depression. I liked my workmates and the banter on site, but their most stimulating conversation at breaktime would be the contents of their sandwiches, how badly Pompey were doing and what was on last night's telly. Not their fault, but mine for leaving school with no other qualification than a swimming certificate and discovering too late that this was not enough of a life for me.

The feeling of being trapped in the wrong job meant the progress and ultimate success of the Rockin' Hot Rods became even more important. Having proper instruments and sound equipment, we could take on proper fee-paying venues, and new gigs included the Clarence Pier and The Parade Hotel on Southsea seafront. In a brief flare of local fame, we would appear on the same bill as the Beatles and other top groups when they played in Portsmouth, but for now we were practising at more modest venues.

We had also seriously stepped up our drug consumption.

Everyday use of drugs in Portsmouth - as elsewhere - is nowadays common. The city has a higher rate of opiate users than average, and one of the highest rates of drug-related death in England.

Not so in our day, and we bad lads were very much an exception. History records that the use of amphetamines started in London around 1960, and reached the provinces a year or so later, some of it courtesy of the notorious and deadly Kray Twins. Before then, altered-state seekers I knew would pop an aspirin into a bottle of Coke, shake it, then glug it down to feel the 'rush'. I also knew a guy who trawled the Southsea pubs, selling what he claimed to be 'reefers' at half a crown a time if he could find a mug or drunken sailor still in funds. His joints were, in fact, hand-rolled cigarettes made from strong tobacco laced with an aspirin or, of all things, gravy browning powder to make a markedly different taste to the normal roll-up. The curious thing was that people who bought and smoked the so-called reefers immediately started to act as if they had indulged in some grade 'A' hippie weed.

We sophisticated rock 'n' roll idols smoked the occasional proper joint, but majored on tabs of what were collectively known as Speed, and in particular French Blues or Purple Hearts. These amphetamine based prescription pills had been introduced to cheer up depressed housewives or people with other reasons to be unhappy, and became known as Mother's Little Helpers after the Rolling Stones' hit of 1967.

The downside of getting high before a show was the lack of attention to the niceties of pace, beat and pitch when getting carried away on stage. After one heavy session at the Clarence Pier, we compared notes in the pub afterwards and found we had been playing in different keys in some numbers, and sometimes even singing and playing different songs.

This may be why we were never invited back to play at the Pier, or it may have been the mass brawl which kicked-off when a music lover threw a glass of stale beer over me during a very mixed finale performance of *Be Bop a Lula*.

~

When I was not amphetamine gigging or rehearsing with the band, the White House had become my home-from-home. It was just over the road, so truly local, and full of people I liked to mix with.

Along with our little gang, my new circle of friends comprised a couple of dozen regulars or irregular regulars who lived locally or further afield. We were a mixed bunch, but we had in common that we came from a working-class background and did manual jobs. I was unusual because my parents owned their home rather than renting council or private accommodation.

Very unusually for those days, there were a number of female regulars who we considered mates, excepting when we lusted after one of them or they made it clear that an approach would be welcomed.

Like the boys, the White House girls came mainly from working-class backgrounds and most earned their wages from factory work.

Also like the boys, the girls were a mixed bunch in appearance and, sometimes, character and attitudes. Some were hardened drinkers and could keep up with the lads and match them for colourful language. Some, like my long-time friend Leslie Gentiles, would even fight like us when the need or inclination arose.

Others were, if not exactly demure, much less outward-going or upfront. One commonality which might surprise anyone under sixty was how most of the apparently freewheeling girls would not think of going into a pub on their own, and that included their local. The routine was that they would pre-arrange an escort, or wait at the door to the Public till one of the boys arrived and escorted them in. Strange indeed to modern ears, but that was how it was.

Our romantic rules of engagement and their outcomes were perhaps not so different from nowadays.

Every now and then, one of the boys would not be seen in the bar during weekdays. This would be either because he was skint, too ill to get out of bed or had formed a meaningful attachment with one of the girls. We would know which girl it was because of her synchronised absences. This would either go on for a week or more before they split up and things got back to normal, or the unthinkable would happen and the couple would not show over the weekend. In these cases, the sequence of events was invariable. In most cases, there would be a parting of the ways and the shamefaced male would reappear at weekends. If his ex returned to her group of mates and the pub, she would be left alone by the boys for a quarantine period. This was not out of sensitivity, but the real risk of violence if her ex-boyfriend objected to any new liaisons, which he usually did.

In rare cases, the couple would stay together and sometimes find a new pub. In even rarer cases they would wed, providing an excuse for some memorable - and often unmemorable - Stag and Hen nights.

~

Because of early starts and financial limitations, The White House would be quiet during the week, and it would be a couple of pints and a game of darts with the boys. In the winter, nothing much happened unless one of us got lucky or there was a free party to gate-crash.

All year round, the weekend was sacred, started on Friday evening and went through to the early hours of Monday morning...sometimes without a break. This mutual belief that not a moment must be wasted meant we had a demanding schedule and timetable, helped by consuming a mixture of a lot of pints and not a few drugs.

Friday night would usually be spent hitting some city-centre pubs before arriving at the Savoy, worse for wear and looking for sex with a stranger or, failing that, a fight with a sailor. But more of that later.

Saturday mornings might see us getting measured

for a new suit at Jacksons or shopping for new gear in Charlotte Street if in funds, or getting a neck shave and all the trims from Al Moody. On a home match day, it would be off to Fratton Park. Unlike the 657 Crew, we did not do away matches, when it would be a curry and chips lunch in the new Indian restaurant just off the Guildhall Square, then the usual Commercial Road parade and pose.

Saturday evening traditionally saw a pleasure trip off the Island, invariably ending with a set-to with the local lads. By now, some of the boys had motors, into which we piled to go as far afield as Brighton, or as close to home as Hayling Island. If we were feeling particularly troublesome, we might visit the Greyhound at Leigh Park or call on the tractor and ploughboys (as we called them) in rural communities like Emsworth and Liphook. The most favoured of us would travel in real style in an American motor with fins that looked as if they could cut an unwary pedestrian in half. The 1958 Plymouth Fury was pillar-box red and belonged to Paul Baron. He was a likeable and obliging young man who had come into an inheritance and was doing his best to spend it before succumbing to the drink he lavished on himself as well as others. Sometimes we would go in convoy to a likely venue, and a popular destination was Haying Island. Apart from The Beach and Ocean Clubs where you could always be sure of a set-to, we would sometimes visit a holiday camp with a novel attraction.

The Kon-Tiki Bar had a Polynesian theme and was kitted out with plastic palm trees and plastic thatching over the bar, on which stood plastic pineapple ice buckets. This was all very trendy, but the centrepiece was a technological marvel that drew admirers from far afield. It took the form of a rigid fibre-glass pond liner, in the middle of which was an artfully constructed tropical island with a tiny volcano in its middle. On the hour and every hour, a hidden propellor would disturb the calm waters, and, lo and behold, the volcano would erupt with smoke and sparks. It may be hard to believe in these days of Computer-Generated Images that people would come from miles around to see the impressive event, but we were obviously a lot easier to please in those far-off days.

~

Another now-shocking aspect of life in the foreign country that was Britain in the Sixties is how socially acceptable it was to drink and drive. And how acceptable it was to drive a death-trap.

The yearly MOT had arrived in 1960, but only tested lighting, steering and braking. The idea of setting a legal limit to how much drivers could drink and testing to see if they were fit to be behind the wheel only came in with the arrival of the breathalyser in 1967. Nowadays is it socially unacceptable to drink or drug drive; in the early years of the decade, the idea of being behind the wheel while tipsy or even blind drunk was quite literally a joke. When a pub regular was so plastered he could hardly stand and someone asked if he would be able to get home safely, the usual response was: 'He'll be fine - he's got the car with him.' The road casualty and death rate at the time reflected the shockingly casual approach to drunk driving. It's a sobering thought that in 1968, nearly 8,000 people were killed on Britain's roads. Nowadays and in spite of the huge increase in traffic, the figure is around 1500. My new group of mates were even more culpable, as we drove under the influence of drugs as well as drink, often both at the same time.

Miraculously, lamp posts, trees and hedges were the most common victims of the insanity, and I survived a dozen potentially fatal collisions when I or another member of the gang was driving. My guardian angel must have been on duty, but not for many others I knew.

A memory that has stayed was the death and funeral of Micky Chapman.

Micky was one of the leading White House Boys, and known for his wit, charm and quick temper. He would have been called a 'likeable rogue' in those days.

It was a normal Friday evening, and I turned up at the White House fully booted and spurred, as we used to say. In prospect were a few beers and then a few drinks on route to the Savoy Ballroom to let the night play out as it would.

As I arrived at the White House I saw Micky emerging from an alleyway. He said he had had a row with his girlfriend, and it was all over. I suggested we go on a pub crawl and drown his sorrows, but he said no. He was going to take his motor and go to Brighton or even Southampton. He asked me to go with him, but I said no, especially if he went to Southampton.

My Friday night took its usual course, but the next day in the White House for a hangover cure, I heard that Micky Chapman had crashed his car on the Eastern Road and was dead.

The small army of mourners met at The White House and followed the hearse on foot to Milton cemetery. As we passed the industrial estate opposite the cemetery, I saw that the windows of every factory overlooking the road were lined by young men and women, paying their respects. Micky Chapman was a well-known figure.

As I looked down into the open grave, I saw from the brass plate on his coffin that Micky had been born within a month of me, and thought how he would never marry, raise a family and have a good, indifferent or bad life.

I wish I could say that the experience had a profound effect on me and changed my approach to risking my and other peoples' lives by drinking and drugging and driving. I'm ashamed to say only age made me see sense.

~

Although the band chose French Blues or Purple Hearts to get us in the mood for a performance, the chemical stimulant of choice at the White House was found in an unlikely setting. Chemists' shops in the area must have thought that there was a long-running epidemic of head colds and blocked noses.

The reason for the sales boom was the discovery that the cardboard strip in a popular brand of decongestant tube was soaked in amphetamine. Nowadays used to treat narcolepsy, ADHD and obesity, Benzedrine was then used to help clear blocked nasal passages. For those in the know, a tube of Nostriline was a lot cheaper than buying 'benny' in tablet form, and would keep the user awake and alert and raring to go for the weekend.

The way of ingesting noz was a matter of choice. Some people tore a piece from the impregnated card and swallowed it down with a draught of beer. Others liked to put it in a stick of chewing gum. However we chose to take it, the intention was the same, to get and stay up for the weekend without losing a minute to sleep.

Nothing is new. Nowadays young people like to take Ecstasy or put white powder up their noses. We used the secret ingredient inside a tube that normal people stuck up their noses to help them breathe more easily.

~

Thanks to the growing success of the band and my adventures with the boys at The White House, my legover rate was climbing nicely. A few years before, I had fallen in love at least once a week. I was a proper teenager in love, and like millions of adolescents, loved the pain of unrequited love. Sitting in my room and listening to a soppy song would move me to tears, even though I had never met my imaginary lover.

Now it was all about lust and not love. Of course, I fancied Cilla, Helen Shapiro, Brenda Lee, Cher and the Ronettes in a distant way, but, like movie stars, they were not real. Selfish creature that I was, I wanted uncomplicated sex, not the responsibility of caring for someone else. Then along came Patsie, the first real love of my life.

We met at a Hot Rod gig and I was more than frustrated that it took me four dates to get inside her bra. To be fair, this was because, as she told me afterwards, she had made the clip unclip-able with sticky tape and wanted to see if I would stick with her despite not being allowed inside her bra or pants.

Eventually, she agreed to let me have my way, and we consummated our relationship in the back garden of a big house in Gosport where the band had been hired to play at a birthday celebration. It was a perfect, balmy summer night, the band had gone down well and we sneaked into a copse at the bottom of the garden with a bottle of fizzy wine. For a change, I took my time and thought of her as well as myself. It was just perfect and I understood for the first time the difference between making love and having sex.

Although I carried on acting like a single man, our love affair was to last for more than a year. It ended when Patsie, who was a couple of years older than me, started to talk about getting engaged. The thought of such commitment terrified me, and at the end of an evening out I told her I wanted to split. I remember walking away and leaving her sitting on the grass in Milton Park. Her head was down, she was tugging at the grass and crying. For the first time in my life, I felt bad about how I had treated a girl.

I still wonder how it would have been had I been man enough to make a commitment and married my Patsie. But then think how that would have meant I would never have met my amazingly tolerant and staunch soul mate, and how our wonderful and unique children and grandsons could never have existed.

~

When bored in the long summer evenings there was always a visit to wind up the Fairground Boys. They tended the arcades and rides and were generally a tough bunch. They were also very protective of their own, and would come running when a bunch of drunken sailors or local yobs kicked off. It was not unusual for punters to be left stranded at the top of the Big Wheel or trapped in a whirling and unattended cage when the action started.

Most of the fairground workers were young, but their natural leader was already middle-aged. Darkie Oakley was a thickset man of middle height and a fearsome performer. I remember once watching as he and Don Price slugged it out, and even the other combatants left off to see the contest. Don, light of weight but fast with his fists as well as on his feet had a natural boxer's action. Darkie just went for his target. I don't know how it ended as I lost interest when something hit me very hard on the side of the head. Afterwards I learned it had been a chain from which hung a score or more keys. It was swung by Big John, the main man in the arcades, and he knew how to use the chain for other things than opening jammed penny slot machines.

I woke up in the toilet block opposite the funfair, where Don had carried me to safety. Inspection showed there was no damage to body or suit, and the only reminder was the dusty outline of Big

John's boot on the side of my face. In later years I reminded him of the incident and we had a drink and a joke, reminisced in mock-heroic terms about past battles and became friends. As I have said before, that happened often in our time.

~

Early summer and I was to make my break for freedom.

One evening after a two-day Ghoster and feeling particularly depressed, I told Mother how unhappy I was and how right she had been about how wrong I had been to leave school early.

She could see how badly I felt and, as usual, came up with a swift and decisive solution.

If I really did not want to spend the rest of my life as a pipe fitter/welder, she could see no point in my carrying on doing something I had begun to hate. I should leave Brightside and look for a part-time job while I studied for and took the examinations for which I had not bothered to sit while at school.

When I said I couldn't just walk away from the job, she said she would win me some time by phoning the company and telling them I had caught a rare and contagious disease from my Uncle Bill. He was a sailor, she would explain, who had just returned from a Far East posting. As usual, Mother was not totally careless with the truth. I did have an Uncle Bill and he was a sailor. He had served in the Far East, but had been home for the past five years.

Mother made the call to the office, ordered the appropriate text books and made enquiries about when and where and how I could sit for GCE qualifications in half a dozen subjects. I put my overalls and knapsack in the shed and prepared to repair the errors of the past.

Thanks to my amazing mum, overnight I had become an unofficial student and, unlike many other things in life, I would get a second chance.

~

By the time I arrived, my new place of employment had had more name changes than my band.

Over preceding years, number 46 Osborne Road had traded three Italian restaurants and a coffee bar called The Keyhole. In the future it would re-brand itself as a very dubious late-night drinking club which was so prone to explode into violence that the beer was sold in plastic glasses. Later still it would become Oysters, a Spanish-type bar comfortably in the experienced hands of my best landlord mate, the wonderful Terry Little. Lurid tales of Fat Charlie Dyke's 'Beastie Bar' abound, and a favourite of mine relates to when I helped Terry clear the premises. In a back room we found a menu blackboard, on which were listed not the dishes of the day, but the cost of varied services provided by the working girls on call. As far as I remember, straight sex was £3, more exotic provisions from £4... and a blow job a fiver.

For now, The Bistro was a frothy coffee and burger establishment, owned by a very large former public school boy and rugger bugger. Charles Pearce (woe betide you if you called him Charlie, or even worse, Chas) lived in a posh flat in Old Portsmouth and spoke like a member of the Royal Family, but as many troublesome customers found out, he was no weak-chinned pushover. He was also very intemperate with customers who liked to linger over their coffee. The house rule was that they had to refill their cups at least once an hour, or hit the road under their own steam or with his assistance.

My job was to chop the onions and cook and serve the burgers, clear the tables and generally help the proprietor keep order. We were at our busiest after the pubs chucked out, and The Bistro became a haven for those who did not want to go home, or had difficulty sleeping because of the amount of noxious substances they had absorbed. I have a crisply clear memory of how the discarded pill bottles crunched under my feet like egg shells as I went about my business.

Even though I was young and Charles was fit, it was hard to keep going all night without assistance, and part of my duties at the start of the evening was to nip next door to the off-licence and buy a small bottle of superstrength Polish vodka. Doled out by the boss at regular intervals, it helped keep our spirits up and eyes open. It also made him even less tolerant, and not a few stroppy customers ended up lying damaged on the pavement outside when they incurred the Wrath of Charles.

The Bistro stayed open until the customers ran out, and it was rare that I finished sweeping up the broken pill bottles and fag ends before dawn broke. The plan had been for me to work at nights at The Bistro and study at home during the day. Like most of my life, the plan didn't work out that way.

~

I was still raising Cain with the Eastney/Milton Boys on my nights off from the Bistro, but also exploring what I hoped was the artistic inner me.

Instead of boning up on the need for isosceles triangles and why it was a sin to split an infinitive, I had begun writing short stories. As part of my plan to move to France and become a bohemian artist, I'd also signed up for a course in Life studies at Portsmouth Art College. I'd assumed it would be about painting bowls of fruit, and only realised that was what they called Still Life when I walked in on a rather large and very naked lady sitting on the floor of the classroom. As our arty-looking female tutor explained, the routine was that we would use our preferred medium and come up with our interpretations of the model.

Most of the class had brought proper art paper and pencils or watercolour paints. Being as ever short of readies, I turned up with a box of charcoal sticks and a roll of patterned wallpaper Mother was not keen on.

I remember clearly how envious I felt when the middle-aged man next to me came up with an almost photographic image of the model. Meanwhile, I had broken several sticks of charcoal and done no more than smear black marks across the blank side of the wallpaper. Somewhere in there was a vaguely human shape, but it looked more like something by Picasso when he was learning the ropes for his Blue Period than the amiable, comfortable and relaxed lady sitting on the cushion.

To my surprise, our tutor was very sniffy about the work by the neat little man with the pencils in his top pocket, but said how impressed she was with my scrawl. She said that (unlike the pencil drawing by my neighbour) my work was full of life and vigour and meaning and revelation. I basked in her praise and realised that being good at painting or drawing in the art world was not good enough. You had to be different, and that suited my lack of talent and ability. I might be rubbish at art, but I was tops at bullshit. A pity, I used to think when miming on stage with the group that the same rules did not apply to the world of music.

~

I suppose a good nickname for me in those days would have been Teflon, as I failed to stick at anything I turned my hand to. If I was not immediately good at it, I'd just walk away. The only exceptions to this general rule were sex and the band.

Predictably, I gave up the art course after a month when our tutor realised my efforts were not bold statements and rejections of the norm, just crap. After sulking for a while, it occurred to me that writers as well as artists had traditionally starved in Parisian garrets, and signed up for a course in creative writing.

The tutor was a thoughtful, writerly-looking chap who had had modest success of his book about being a military policeman in Palestine after the War. He did his best to get me to understand why it was wrong to end a sentence with a preposition or commit assault and battery on something called syntax, but again I failed to stick at it. Flatteringly, both the art and writing tutors wrote to ask me to return as they and their class members missed my valuable and entertaining contributions. It was flattering, but I suspect the truth was that they wanted to keep their numbers up, and my contributions were mostly giving the rest of the class a laugh with my weird drawings and mangled sentences.

~

My apprenticeship as a pipe fitter/welder was another of the few things I was to stick at, but that was because it turned out I had no choice.

A law passed in 1563 made it illegal for anyone to "...exercise any Art, Mystery or Occupation within the realm of England except he shall have been brought up at least seven years as an apprentice." There were strict penalties for anyone who broke the rules, and especially for any indentured youth who tried to break his apprenticeship. As I was to find, things had not changed that much by my part of the 20th century.

My mother had bluffed our way through the first fortnight by phoning the office and telling them I was still suffering from the exotic ailment passed on by my Uncle Bill.

But in those days doctors were much harder to bluff, and without a sick note, she couldn't keep the deception going.

I remember that the general manager - a round little man with a moustache and a look of the popular comedian Arthur Haynes - was sympathetic to my situation, and said he had always wondered why I had chosen to go on the tools rather than take the comfortable job in the office I had been offered.

Whatever I had said at the time, he said, he had not seen me being happy as a pipe fitter. But it was too late now. There were severe financial penalties if I refused to complete my indentures.

With an encouraging pat on my shoulder, he made a bad pun about me looking on the bright side, and said that there were after all, less than three years to go as an apprentice. In the meantime, I could continue to study in my spare time and get some academic qualifications under my belt. Having, as it were, done my time, I would be free to leave the trade and start a more suitable career.

I listened to what he had to say, thanked him for his time and went and sat in the nearest pub and thought about my options. I could refuse to return to work, but I could not expect my parents to pay the breathtakingly high cost of my breaking my agreement with Brightside. Then I thought about doing a runner, stowing away on a ferry and finding a garret in Montmartre to rent. There I would spend my evenings in the local zinc bars, discussing Art and Life with my fellow painters over a glass or two of absinthe.

There were, on reflection, several drawbacks to that plan. Firstly, my parents would still have to pay the financial penalty, and cutting and running would mean leaving the band and missing out on future fame and fortune. There was also the consideration that I was as useless at painting as I was at holding a tune.

In the end I ordered another pint, phoned my mother, and then the manager. I would, as he suggested, return and do my time, while studying for a brighter future.

~

Back in harness, the weather made my return to the building site at least bearable. It also made time off so much more precious, and the summer of 1962 was to be long, hot and memorable.

Most sunny Saturdays would see our gang gathered at a part of Southsea beach we had made our own. Our chosen spot was known locally as The Snake Pit, which seemed somehow suitable when we were present. We would laze around all day, the boys dashing down the beach in our Speedo-type budgie smugglers or underpants if we had forgotten them, stomachs held in to impress the girls with a few powerful strokes in the shallows before our lungs gave out. Unless paired off, The White House Girls would strip to their frilly one-piece bathing suits or a then quite daring bikini and flirt with any good-looking boys who had the nerve to respond.

Then, when the weather favoured us, it became the fashion to spend the entire weekend on a foreign beach. Package tours to Spain and other sunny climes were not too far into the future, but for then it was a fairly dirty weekend on Hayling Island.

We would meet at South Parade pier and catch the open-top bus to ride along the promenade, then walk with bags and tents along Ferry Road, the boys pointing out the spots on the Humps and Bumps where they claimed to have scored.

It was the shortest of boat rides to the westerly tip of Hayling Island, where we would set up camp amongst the sand dunes. There was a pub nearby, and the boys would collect driftwood and some-times bits of the wooden fence marking out the boundaries of the golf links.

With the fire going and as the sun set over Portsmouth and the sky filled with stars, we were kings, and would savour and long remember joys of youth and fitness and irresponsibility. As warriors have done across the millennia, the boys would sit around the fire and tell tales of encounters and victories which got more improbable as the scrumpy went down. The unattached girls would visit the pub in their skimpy beach wear to drive the local men wild with lust, then return to feast on baked potatoes and sausages cooked over the fire. For the while, the world was ours and it was good to be young and strong and free. We did not know what the future held, but knew it would have to go some to beat those long, lazy weekends on the shore.

~

As I was shortly to discover, not all those beach party weekend had happy outcomes.

As well as drinking gallons of rough cider and a tube or two of noz, the boys would be on the lookout for any pretty girls on the loose. Some might be camping amongst the dunes, or to be found in the local pub. Some were available, and I found one who was much too available.

After a brief encounter in a wartime concrete bunker near the pub, I had a very nasty shock a few days later. I was looking in the bathroom mirror as I worked on my quiff and was stunned to see that my eyebrows seemed to be moving of their own volition.

Looking closer, I was horrified to see they appeared

to be teeming with a host of tiny green crabs. Then I found the creatures making them-selves at home in the hair under my armpits and around my willy pubic hair. In a panic, I found and confided in a mate who had spent his National Service with a medical unit. He took one look at my moving eyebrows and said I had picked up a dose of pubic lice, or as we knew them, crabs. They could be picked up from toilet seats or even towels, but most usually from close contact with another body. Rather than go to the doctor, he said that the DIY method was to shave the hair off all the effected parts and paint them with iodine.

That night I locked myself in the bathroom, shaved where necessary and noted that my pubic area now looked like a plucked chicken with a very short neck. I then prepared to administer the iodine, but pressed too hard on the rubber bulb and sent a stream on to the tip of my penis. It was, to say the least, painful, and drew attention from Mother. I gritted my teeth and told her I had nicked myself while shaving.

Until my eyebrows grew back, I explained my dark glasses by claiming to have suffered from arc eyes, a painful condition resulting from looking at the spark while welding with the naked eye. There was no explaining away my yellow-tinted shaved chicken's neck, so had to abstain from sex for a fortnight. At that time, it seemed almost an eternity.

~

Another possible escape route from a life of slog and boredom on the building sites, and for a while I thought I could be a real contender: I would fight for money and not just fun. The proposal came from my friend Don Price, he of the flashing fists and big smile.

Don was the result of a fleeting wartime union between a local girl and a visiting USA soldier, over to practise for the D-Day Landings. The soldier was black, and despite his mixed-race parentage, so was Don. Perhaps the reason he was so good with his fists was the need to protect his body and dignity in those days of casual and ubiquitous racism.

I honestly don't remember my daily life being full of incidents involving hate crime or speech, but then people took offence less easily then, probably because they had little choice. Also there did not seem to be a lot of differently coloured or sexually oriented people about then. There were lots of mostly Bangladeshi owners and workers in what we called Indian restaurants, a small clique of very outré gay men on the seamier pub circuit, and we were very much not welcome in the couple of tough boozers where openly butch lesbians wore their cropped hair, tattoos and boots. Also, I think it's important to remember that we were equally-ist or phobic to everyone who did not conform to our idea of a norm. People lacking teeth were known to their friends as 'Gummy' or 'Gabby', or 'Fang' if they had only one or two. Short people were called 'lofty', overweight males and females might be known as 'Fatty Arbuckle' or 'Two Ton Tessie'. Those with remarkable facial or other features and even disabilities were not immune from casual sobriquet like Limpy, Gimpy or Hopalong if they had a club foot (as it was then known) or less than the normal complement of legs. People with thin faces and sticky-out ears would always be 'Wingnut', and people with oversized noses would be Shonky, or nicknamed for a well-known person with a large proboscis. I remember an otherwise lovely barmaid at one of our locals who had a rather large nose. She was known as 'Cyril' and never knew that this was because of the equally nasally enhanced Pompey footballer, Cyril Rutter. Girls with big breasts would be known as Titsolina or Twiggy. There were all sorts of other nicknames which today would be classed as 'hate speech'. To be fair, we were evenly-handed in our everyday-ismness, and would be equally rude to anyone from north of the Watford Gap or of Welsh, Scots or Irish lineage - and especially anyone who came from Southampton.

However much that might horrify those with modern sensibilities, it was how it was and you had to take it or make it known you were not happy about being labelled. Though extremely overweight at primary school and my early years at the Technical High School, I was rarely bullied or teased because of my size. I don't think this was because of the sensitivity of my schoolmates, but more because of my readiness to give the offender something to think about.

No matter how rife, and it was, I was aware of prejudice and bigotry, and I think that's why I sought Don Price's friendship. Not because I felt bad about the way people would think less of him because of the colour of his skin. And certainly not because I wanted to do any early virtue-signalling. Apart from him being such an honest and decent and friend-worthy man, I wanted to be close to Don in the same way I liked being friends with foreigners, gays, alcoholics, drug addicts and disabled people. They were different, and I liked differentness.

~

Though council house blocks and towers still define Portsea, they rub shoulders with million-pound apartments that have a not much better view of the sea. Tapas and sushi bars are common, and, ironically, tattooists have had a rebirth by marking the skins of women and fashion-conscious males rather than drunken sailors.

Close to the main Dockyard gates, Queen Street was for centuries the natural location for tattooists, drug dens, taverns and other houses of ill-repute. In our day, it was still a pretty dodgy thoroughfare, and we would not have ventured into one of the boozers owned by the Portsea Boys without invitation or permission.

Queen Street was also the setting for the Portsea Rotary Boxing Club, and where Don Price and I arrived three times a week to train.

It had been Don's idea that I join him as an active member, and I suspect it was because he had seen how badly I defended myself in a bundle. Or perhaps he just wanted some company. For whatever reason he suggested it, I liked the idea of learning how to defend myself in the traditional way, and especially how cool it looked running back-wards along Southsea prom while bobbing and weaving and punching an imaginary opponent.

Portsea Rotary was not much to look at, but known for accomplished and title-winning local fighters as

Brian Sandy, 'Bomber' Mellish and Ray Daniels. Our usual routine was that Don would spar with others in his light-middleweight division, while I would be put in to spar with the smallest boxers. This was to get them used to a heavy punch, and help me learn to be quicker on my feet and with my guard. It was at Portsea that I leaned that a knock-out punch was all about timing and not enthusiasm.

Being so rubbish, I was very surprised when Don and I were approached by a former cruiserweight champion who wanted to become our manager. Thinking about it, probably it was like my relationship with the band. I came as part of the package, regardless of my lack of talent.

The owner of a coal delivery company, John Smith had been around the boxing game for a long time, and looked it. He was in fact a gentle man, and helped many a boy from a very deprived back-ground escape from the inevitable journey from poverty to violent crime.

After a month, Johnny declared we were ready to represent the club, and we were included in a team taking on the inmates at an Approved School on the Isle of Wight. 'Approved' meant the pupils were deemed to be beyond parental control, had committed a crime and were too young to go to prison or the tougher Borstal system.

I remember sitting on the ferry with Don and John, yawning repeatedly as I looked out of the Solent. I may have looked relaxed, but yawning before a fight is a sure sign of trepidation.

My opponent was a tall, stringy youth called Toogood, and so he proved to be.

I was resplendent in black tee-shirt, golden shorts

and impressive white boxing boots on loan from John Smith. In contrast, Master Toogood wore almost knee-length, baggy, patched shorts and black plimsolls. I remember noticing how his big toe stuck out through a hole in one.

The difference between our appearances was marked, and some wag in the audience dubbed me The Black Knight. Warming up in my corner to cheers and jeers, I have to say I looked the business, but once again I proved to be all show and little go.

For the first round, I stuck to the tactics John had taught me, bobbing and weaving and concentrating on holding my hands high and feeling my opponent out with the occasional straight jab or attempted dig to the ribs. Obviously, nobody had taught Mr Toogood the way to box, and he came straight at me like a maddened bull.

Halfway through the second round, I lost my cool, dropped all thoughts of technique, put my head down and went for him with flailing fists.

The result was obviously not to the satisfaction of the crowd, and there was much booing when my opponent was awarded the match on points.

I boarded the ferry and went home with a black eye, bruised lip and ego, and a burning sense of injustice, and a week later hung up my gloves.

When summer had flown and the weather turned, our winter night routine for Friday evenings would start at the heart of the city.

Before the War, it was said no sailor had been known to take just half a pint of beer in each pub in Commercial Road and reach the end of his journey under his own steam. Thanks to the Luftwaffe and redevelopment, many of the most notorious pubs in the city centre have since been replaced with nail parlours or trendy coffee shops, but some have survived with a change of name and image.

For us, Friday night trawl of the Commercial Road pubs wasn't complete without a visit to The Albany.

One of the Victorian 'gin palaces' built to entice working men to spend their wages before staggering home with empty pockets, the Albany was as overblown as its beer was rotten and its customers colourful. Outside it promised much with its soaring, grand façade; inside, below a lofty ceiling was a long, high bar and cubicles of elaborately carved dark wood and engraved glass.

In spite of the bad beer (tainted by the scrumpy cider) the Albany was a popular pub, and more so when the Fleet was in. Entertainment counted for more than the quality of the ale, and there was always something happening at the Club Albany, as it was known at ports around the world.

Sailors on a runashore were easy to spot as their choice of civilian gear was almost as consistent as their uniforms. Waylaid by one of the 'smutter' vans which would be lying in wait like the local tarts at the Dockyard gates, the typical rating sported a coloured blazer with silver buttons and a crown motif on the breast pocket. The shirt would be white and the slim-jim tie was an almost compulsory red. Grey, sta-prest trousers and black 'winklepicker' shoes completed the ensemble. Another giveaway of the wearer's occupation would be the contrast of a long quiff or Beatle fringe above a short back-and-sides.

Other regular patrons of The Albany would include local lads like us, minor criminals and pedlars of stolen goods, sightseers, the occasional totter with or without his horse, and always a selection of the city's working girls.

They were as easily spottable as out-of-uniform matelots, and we knew them all. There was Josie, Jan, Julie and the scar-faced Gloria. Although she did not turn me on, Gloria had a glass eye, and the story went that she lost the original after luring a drunken sailor on to a patch of waste ground behind the pub. Her pimp was lying in wait to roll the skate, as the popular practice was known, but was so pissed he missed the target and hit Gloria with the broken bottle. It was said that she turned the incident to her favour by telling potential customers she would keep an eye out for them.

Head girl was, as she was known, Big Fat Sylvie. She was indeed a large lady, invariably clad in a voluminous fake leopard skin coat. I once asked her if she was never scared to go down a dark alley with a stranger. She smiled almost contemptuously and snapped open her matching leopard skin handbag to show me the long kitchen knife inside. It was, she said, looking at my crotch, for little boys who got lairy and needed a trim.

The most legendary of all the city's working girls was one I never met.

According to some sources, Pompey Lil began servicing the needs of the Fleet in the early years of the 20th century. If true and she were still around in my time, she would have been well beyond retirement age. Or perhaps she had handed the baton and name to a younger woman or even a relative. Or perhaps she never really existed, which would be a shame. Part of the Pompey Lil legend was that she had no teeth, which made one of her services particularly appealing.

~

Despite being a naval port, I don't remember a significant number of gay men or women on the pub and club scene.

That lack of overt gayness may have been because the practice of acts of homosexuality was, hard to believe as it may be, illegal till 1967. Acts of what was called gross indecency between men could result in a prison sentence of two years.

The excuse for beating someone up in a toilet because they had propositioned you was actually known around the world as The Portsmouth Defence.

I'm sure there were places where homosexual men and women gathered, but most gay men kept their sexuality to themselves for fear of ridicule at best. As for gay women, it was difficult for us red-blooded males to believe that any female would prefer the attention of another woman.

Two exceptions to the rule and regulars at The Albany and other city centre pubs were Little Wally and Peter the Pouffe.*

As his nickname suggests, Wally the Woofter was short and slight of stature. He was fine of features with a halo of wispy hair, and I remember his delicate hands, which he used expressively when telling a risqué story or making a more than usually outrageous proposition. He habitually wore a truly voluminous pink mohair sweater, and supplemented whatever income he had by collecting and washing-up glasses at a number of pubs. Some landlords were obviously sympathetic and soft-hearted; others saw his value as an attraction to a certain type of customer. For sure, Wally was a natural entertainer, but he was nowhere near as renowned as Peter the Pouffe.

Peter was of middle years, swarthy and sported a prominent mole on one cheek. I seem to remember he displayed it as a beauty spot. He perennially wore jeans and either a sweater or donkey jacket, and I never saw him without a greasy Breton-style cap. He was wiry but very strong and capable, as any number of runashore sailors or stag night members found out during his active years. I don't know if he had a regular job or how else he may have earned a living, but he was part of the mix which made Portsmouth such a colourful and memorable place in those still repressed times.

Once seen in action, he was rarely forgotten, especially when performing his famed Bottle Dance. I will go no further than saying it involved a large bottle of Forest Brown Ale, bought for him and placed on the floor by a spectator and involving the lowering of his jeans.

I don't know how he did it, but the cap was always missing when he stood up and retrieved the bottle.

*I would like to again re-reiterate that some of the expressions and attitudes above were, like me, of their time. If they offend any reader I am sorry, but to change the language and expressions to suit modern sensibilities would be to defeat the point of writing the book.

Having warmed up in the city centre, the five of us would cram into a cab and make for Southsea seafront. We were beyond the maximum payload for taxis, but few drivers were going to refuse our business, and we got to where we were going for a tanner apiece (2.5 p)

There was only one place to be and be seen on a Friday night for anyone in Southsea. Liverpool had its Cavern Club, and Manchester the Hacienda. Pompey had the Savoy Ballroom. There was also the Mecca in the city centre, but that was off-limits for us Southsea dwellers.

Across the road from South Parade Pier and now yet another trendy development of eye-wateringly expensive apartments, the Savoy hit its heyday after the War, and was a venue for big-name bands like Ted Heath and Joe Loss and their orchestras. Big bands ruled till the beginning of the Sixties, when the legendary Savoy manager George Turner saw that times were changing. Jazz bands led by Acker Bilk, Chris Barber and Kenny Ball drew huge audiences. Then it was the turn of top solo pop stars like Marty Wilde, Billy Fury and Vince Eager. Later, chart-topping acts included The Rolling Stones, The Kinks and The Beatles. My band was to act as backing group for a number of top names, and played our last gig there. But that came later, and for now, I would join many hundreds of young people to dance, drink and, sometimes, fight the night away.

~

On Fridays, four bob (20p) was the price of entry to The Savoy. Provided, that was, that you got past the door stewards, as bouncers were then known.

Girls were always welcome, and as long as we were smartly dressed and not currently banned, so were we lads. Providing, of course, we passed the Collar Test. This involved being scrutinised from behind by a doorman on each side as we shuffled towards the ticket kiosk. The biggest and most extravagant quiffs were acceptable, but if a single hair on the back of a neck touched the collar, the wearer was refused admission and escorted off the premises. There was no appeal, and the rule was not a problem for sailors, but it was for people with, like me, short necks. That's one of the reasons that the High Boston Neck Shave was such a popular choice from legendary barbers like Al Moody.

~

Once inside, we'd make straight up the wide staircase and then up again to the bar on the gallery. I remember that some draught beers were served from a long, flexible pipe with a nozzle you would more likely expect to find at a petrol station. The barman would squirt Bass into the five glasses lined up on the bar, and we would make for the balcony outside.

A decade earlier, the scene below would have been of stiffly-dressed couples gliding across the floor to waltzes and even a daring tango. Now it was our turn, and beat music was king.

There would be girls with flouncy dresses and skirts whirling and a smartly-suited partner, often acting as no more than a prop. Sometimes, the male partner would be an accomplished bopper, showing off his paces and earning admiring looks from the girls lining the dance floor and scowls from we non-participants. Later it would become cool to strut your stuff, but then it was seen as too undignified for us lads to take to the floor. The truth was that, apart from an awkward attempt at The Twist after a few shants, most of us couldn't dance and were content to watch and drink. I was ahead of the game as, though I would never admit it to my mates, I regularly practised bopping moves and techniques in my bedroom. My partner would be the doorknob, and I got adept at spinning round or falling backwards or jumping in the air and always catching my imaginary partner's hand as she completed a twirl.

Sometimes there would be action on the first floor when a fight broke out. Most were between sailors and civilians, and started in the bar. Like western movie saloon brawls, they were often spectacular but usually caused little harm except to glasses and the odd chair or table. I remember one of the boys leaving half an ear on the floor of the bar, but that was an exceptional event. Generally, the scraps were almost part of the entertainment, and girls would enjoy screaming as the bouncers piled in and the band played on.

~

As chucking-out time neared, we would drain our glasses, straighten our ties and try to repair the ravages of a boozy and sometimes battling evening.

Outside, we would grab a burger (sixpence with or

without onions) from the takeaway next door to the entrance, and wait to try our luck as the Savoy emptied.

Emboldened by at least a gallon of beer, the routine would be to accost any remotely attractive girl and ask where she lived. If interested, she might tell you, and her answer would depend on whether or not you offered to walk her home. If she lived south of Fratton Bridge, you would make the offer. If further north, you would make your excuses and try again.

More often than not, it was a lonely walk home to end the big night out.

My generation were regularly bored by hearing our grandfathers talk of a night on the town, supping well and coming home with a fish and chip supper and change from half a crown (12p). Things had changed by the early Sixties, but not that much. I would take a pound note with me on a Friday night, and expect to wake up in the morning with a hangover and handful of clods (copper coins) on the bedside table. Sometimes there would be a charge sheet with them, which did not help with the hangovers.

~

After the pubic hair crab's incident, another painful encounter, and perhaps just desserts for my unconfined promiscuity.

I met the small girl with the elfin face and haircut and very large breasts at the funfair, and we ended up hours later in a mate's bedsit in Goldsmith Avenue.

Very unusually for those times she had tattoos on

her upper arms and inside her thighs. One was a badly done representation of an erect penis, pointing the way to the shadowy area between her legs. I suppose this should have been a warning sign, but lust is blind.

Another clue came when she seemed strangely reluctant to get down to it, and smothered my willy with what I took to be hand cream. I flattered myself that she was making entry easier for my oversized willy, which meant she must have been having sex with some very poorly endowed men. Actually and as I was to shortly learn, the poor girl was trying to prevent me from catching what she knew she had.

The sharp lesson came a few days later, when I felt a burning sensation as I peed,

Then, to my horror, a yellow, pus-like fluid put in an appearance.

After consulting with an experienced mate known as VD Vic, I arrived at a series of bolted-together portacabins in the grounds of St Mary's Hospital. Looking through a window I recognised one of the working girls from the Albany, so knew I was in the right place.

The young doctor was quite matter-of-fact when he told me I had managed to pick up a venereal disease technically known as gonorrhoea and in the trade as The Clap. When he said I would feel a little prick, I said I already did, then saw the large hypodermic syringe and closed my eyes.

Afterwards, I zipped up and the man in the white coat said I would be okay, but I would need to keep my pecker in my pants for a while, hard though it might be.

~

Another change in line-up and yet another name as the Rockin' Hot Rods metamorphosed into The Stormriders.

By now, my band was getting to be like a company which goes bust, changes the name and sets up again. As well as names, there had been a lot of changes in the line-up. By my reckoning, in less than three years we'd got through two bass guitarists, three drummers, five vocalists and half a dozen lead guitarists. I was the only constant, and suspected it might be me and my attitude causing so many members to jump ship. To be fair, most were poached by or found places in groups which were doing better than us. Inadvertently, I had become manager of a training camp which groomed talented beginners, then lost them.

Our new guitarist was an unlikely rock musician and could hardly be more unlike Tony Nabarro in appearance and attitude to life. A neat, shy and thoughtful man given to modest hairstyles; Barry Roberts looked more like a schoolteacher than a lead guitar player.

When we met and he said he would like to learn to play the guitar, I gave him some tips on where to buy a starter model, together with my copy of the Shadows huge hit, *Apache*. A week later, I called at his bedsitter to see how he was getting on, and from what I heard through the door, it sounded as if he was holding Hank B Marvin hostage. I signed him up on the spot and his dedication was evident when I saw the copy of *Apache* I had loaned him to practise on had been played so many times the grooves had turned white.

The other new band member replaced Eric Smith, who had replaced Sean Conlan. Eric had good looks and a good voice and, even better, had a van we could use to transport our kit. As he was a butcher, the inside of the van was a bit ripe and there was a risk of getting blood and sawdust on our instruments. Eric also suffered badly from eczema and mostly performed with bandaged hands. We made a virtue of it by getting him to wear black gloves like Gene Vincent, but his ailment grew worse and he left.

Yet another line-up for the band: Note my secret smile as apart from the other members of the group, I am the only one who knows my guitar is not plugged in and I am miming.

Our new front man was Bert Parker, a meaty chap with a round face, pointy nose, big teeth and smile and a big quiff of violently blond hair. He had a powerful voice and engaging manner and, coincidentally like Eric, worked at a butcher's shop. Unfortunately he didn't drive, but offered to help with the transport problem by taking as much of our kit as he could manage to gigs in the basket and panniers on his delivery bike.

~

An already eventful year was drawing to its close, and I experienced my first night in custody.

Five of us shared a cell in the tiny police station in Milton, not a hundred yards from our local pub. We were there because of a scrimmage at The Oyster House, a pub at the bottom of Locksway Road.

As was not uncommon, I was the catalyst. A week earlier I had been involved in a verbal confrontation with someone at the Savoy. I had heard he was a policeman who liked to provoke young men and then pull out his warrant card and arrest them. I do not know if this was true, but we met again in the hall behind the pub, and a mass brawl ensued. The scene was attended by a large number of policemen, and I was arraigned for trial for causing an affray and imposing actual bodily harm on the off-duty officer.

Nobody was more surprised than me when I was cleared, and the policeman left the area and took up a post in an overseas British Dominion.

~

The postscript to the affair came some weeks later when I was accosted by a couple of large uniformed officers when I was leaving the Savoy. One of them was holding a large, slavering German Shepherd on a slack leash. Although I was for once innocent of any offence or ill-doing, they bundled me in a van without a word and took me to the police station in Albert Road. There, I was put in a cell and left to stew until a uniformed inspector arrived. He took off his tunic, rolled up his sleeves, then took a large key from his pocket. He turned and locked the cell door, then put the key back in his pocket.

As he walked towards where I sat on the bunk, he said that I had caused a good policeman to have to leave the Force and the country; if I could get past him, I could have the key and walk free from the station.

I like to think I didn't put up much of a defence simply because I was being attacked by a senior police officer. More likely he was too much for me, and the engagement was brief. The cell door was unlocked, I was taken to the toilets and my face washed clean of blood, then to an office where my assailant sat behind his desk. Obviously one with a liking for dramatic gestures, he pushed two A4 sized pieces of paper across the desk and invited me to choose one. They couldn't bring me to the station and let me go without a charge he said, especially with a bruised face; the choice was between Obstruction or Obscene Language. He advised me that the bad language charge carried a lesser penalty, and he would go easy in his evidence.

I took the Obscene Language, and the Inspector did indeed go easy on me when he (unusually) gave evidence at my court appearance. He said that the defendant (he called me 'George') had obviously had a drink too many and had sworn at two officers when leaving the Savoy ballroom. When asked what exactly I had said, he solemnly wrote on a piece of paper, which the court usher showed me and then the Magistrate. It read:

'Why can't you fucking coppers leave me alone?'

The Magistrate was Mrs Mack, a severe - looking lady of late-middle age in a pill-box hat who I knew to be the proprietor of an ex-WD goods and garments shop in Charlotte Street I noted that her eyebrows twitched when it was her turn to read my alleged words, then she looked up and asked me if I had, in fact, said them.

I nodded, and she looked gravely at me as if about to don the Black Cap and sentence me to be hanged by the neck until dead. In fact, she handed me a fine of £2 and cautioned that I should be more respectful to the Police, who were after all only trying to do their job.

This was to be my first conviction, the next being not long after, and for the offence I had turned down in the Inspector's office. In truth and as with the Obscene Language charge, I was innocent. I'd been standing on the wide pavement outside my former place of employment, The Bistro, when a couple of large uniforms arrived and told me to move on. When I asked why, they said I was obstructing the highway. I said words to the effect that I was not, and there was a *déjà vu* return to the police van and visit to Albert Road. This time I was not beaten up, but charged with refusing to move on when asked.

As I ascended to the dock, I realised it was my, by now, regular Magistrate Mrs Mack, She was wearing what looked like the same pill-box hat, and when she looked up and saw me, she said in a stage whisper to the Clerk of the Court: 'I've had this man up before me recently, should I still sit on his case in case of prejudice?'

He assured her it was okay, and I reflected it was a good job there was not a jury to be influenced by her stage whisper. After a very short reprise of the alleged events, Mrs Mack accepted my plea of guilty, then handed me a fine of £4, followed by another lecture about not picking on policemen.

The above incidents are as true as my recollection has recorded them. I suppose I could say that they embittered or soured me and my views of the police service and those who served in it.

Actually, I believe I got what I deserved, and though innocent of these two very minor charges, was guilty of dozens more, most of which went unpunished.

It's an irony that any one of my convictions for violence broke the terms of my apprenticeship, so I could have been sacked and thus won freedom from my ties to the company.

Author's Note: It only occurred to me as I recorded these memories just what a lot of punch-ups, set-tos and general acts of violence I was involved in (and often started) during this year. Every blow, escapade and incident described happened, though some circum-stances and names have been changed for obvious reasons. In fact, I've left out many more altercations than those I've chronicled, probably because I am now ashamed of my part in them. I have no excuse for my behaviour, which, now I think about it, had little to do with anger, aggression or confrontation. It was all about gaining and maintaining a reputation with other young men (and women) as a tough guy.

Apart from the few occasions when I was attacked and had to defend myself, it was mostly about looking for trouble and never backing down from a challenge no matter how scared I was. Like a gunslinger in the Old West, once I'd gained my reputation, I had to literally fight to keep it. As to why it mattered to me and all those other young men at this time and throughout the ages, you would need to ask a psychiatrist. I think perhaps it was and is all to do with the animal kingdom and what was implanted in us before we became 'civilised'. The biggest or best fighters kept their territory and got the girl. That's only my theory, of course.

1963

~ French President Charles de Gaulle vetoes Britain's entry into the European Common Market

~ The Beatles record their debut album *Please, Please Me* at the Abbey Road Studios

~ In Paris, six men are sentenced to death for an assassination attempt on President de Gaulle. Five are pardoned, the sixth is shot.

~ Race Riots take place in Dudley in the West Midlands

~ The second James Bond film *From Russia with Love* is released

~ The first episode of *Dr Who* is screened by the BBC

~ US country music superstar Patsy Cline is killed in a plane crash in Tennessee

~ The Great Train Robbery takes place in Buckinghamshire

~ Dr Richard Beeching's report calls for massive cuts to the rail network

~ The Beatles make their first appearance in Portsmouth

~ 70,000 marchers arrive in London to protest against nuclear weaponry

~ The final servicemen are released as Conscription (The Call-Up) ends

- ~ Kim Philby is named as the Third Man in the Burgess/Maclean spy scandal
- ~ The MP John Profumo/Christine Keeler Scandal hits the headlines
- ~ US President John Kennedy is assassinated in Dallas, Texas
- ~ Portsmouth man George East changes his hairstyle

Top Tunes from British Artists

Please, Please Me ~ The Beatles
Lucky Lips ~ Cliff Richard and the Shadows
You'll Never Walk Alone ~ Gerry and the Pacemakers
Atlantis ~ The Shadows
Just Like Eddie ~ Heinz
Sukiyaki ~ Kenny Ball and his Jazzmen
Charmaine ~ The Bachelors
Go Away Little Girl ~ Mark Wynter
It Only Took a Minute ~ Joe Brown and the Bruvvers
Diamonds ~Jet Harris and Tony Meehan
When Will I Say I Love You ~ Billy Fury
I Who Have Nothing ~ Shirley Bassey
Up On the Roof ~ Kenny Lynch
Hello Little Girl ~ The Fourmost
I Only Want to Be with You ~ Dusty Springfield
I'll Keep You Satisfied ~ Billy J Kramer and the Dakotas
Loop-de-Loop ~ Frankie Vaughan
Island of Dreams ~The Springfields
Do You Love Me ~ Brian Poole and the Tremolos
You were Made for Me ~ Freddie and the Dreamers
Glad All Over ~ The Dave Clark Five
Sugar and Spice ~ The Searchers
Confessin' That I Love You ~ Frank Ifield
Secret Love ~ Kathy Kirby

You say that you love me (Say you love me)
All of the time (All of the time)
You say that you need me (Say you need me)
You'll always be mine (Always be mine)
I'm feelin' glad all over
Yes, I'm-a glad all over
Baby, I'm glad all over
So glad you're mi-i-i-ne

Glad All Over by The Dave Clark Five. Lyrics by
Dave Clark and Mike Smith

Thanks to the success of the North End Snooker
Club, we were returning to Southsea, and in some
style.

The club was thriving because of a combination of
my dad's likeability and Mother's business acumen.
The mouldy meat pies had been replaced with filled
rolls and for the first time in the club's history there
was a daily lunchtime special. New baize cloths had
replaced the moth-eaten originals on all seven
tables, which had also been levelled up so the balls
would run straight and true. This disappointed the
sharks who had taken full advantage of knowing
which way the balls were going to run off, but it
pleased the hordes of new members.

The premises had been generally tarted up, and
even the toilet had had a makeover and was almost
odour-free. This displeased some of the older
regulars, who said the place didn't have the same
atmosphere.

Most importantly of all, the biggest increase in

turnover and net profit came from the one-armed bandits.

Being a lifelong betting man, my dad understood how gamblers thought, and he had a perfect partner in Johnny Haynes. John was a likeable and energetic young man who rented fruit machines and juke boxes to pubs and clubs across the city. Every week he would come to the club out of hours to check the machines were behaving themselves and set to take the maximum profit. They were not rigged to cheat the punter, but set to give the best percentage return, which was a crucial consideration. If the machines didn't pay out regularly, they would not be played. John and dad also ensured the machines offered the biggest jackpots, and made a lot of noise when they paid out a cascade of shiny coins. Serious punters would sit and watch the Mountain Climber for days until they figured it had been primed enough to be due a pay-out.

Because the family finances were doing so well, dad had awarded himself a new second-hand car - a magnificent 1947 Alvis - and a couple of greyhounds to race at the local track. Mother had bought herself and us a new home.

I think she regretted moving from Kay's Stores to the little house in Milton, and couldn't bear the thought of living anywhere that wasn't making money. Accordingly, she had bought a huge, rambling detached house in Southsea in which our previous home and Kay's Stores would have fitted with rooms to spare.

Number 34, St Edwards Road had once belonged to a Victorian Lord Mayor of Portsmouth, and was as grand as his status demanded.

Round the corner from the home of my heart in Castle Road, the house had eight bedrooms and reception rooms to spare, all spread across its three-and-a-half floors. At the end of the garden, an unusually large garage opened on to a lane holding a handful of very desirable, tucked-away homes.

Dad liked the idea of having a big garage to keep his Alvis in, and Mother liked the idea of having a roomy, self-contained garden flat to let out.

The house was in pretty good condition, and you could have held tea dances in the giant drawing room. As to the price of this very grand house, we may need a trigger warning here for younger readers struggling to get on to the housing ladder.

The asking price was, I remember, a shade over £2,500, which at the time seemed to me to be a lot of money to pay just for a house.

A bonus for me was that, apart from being back in my beloved Southsea, I got a suite of rooms to myself. They were at the very top of the house and made from what would have been the attic. The sloping ceiling of one of the rooms was lined with cupboards, in which I found a treasure trove of items left behind after the sale. There was a magnificent model sailing ship, a shiny top hat in its own carrying case, a set of leather-bound engineering manuals and a 'thunderbox' mobile commode made for officers on the move in India at the time of The Raj. There were also three foggy watercolours by the then unappreciated local artist William Edward Atkins. They hang on the wall of our sitting room now, and I suppose they are currently valued at many times what Mother paid for the

Pride and Joy: Dad's beloved Alvis, complete with chauffeur.

house I found them in.

The reason I had two rooms to play with was that brother John was still away at sea.

Having finished his pipe-fitting apprenticeship, he had wanted to see more of the world than the building sites of Hampshire. Having inherited the family gift for verbal embroidery, he had talked himself into the post of Fifth Engineer aboard a ship preparing to circumnavigate the world. The MV Arthur was commonly known as a tramp steamer, picking up and dropping off all manner of goods from port to port in far-flung and often exotic locations. As John said, he did not know one end of a piston shaft from another, but there were four other officers to ask for help if something went wrong on his shift.

Always a good and thoughtful son, he wrote regularly with lengthy descriptions of his adventures, and Mother treasured every word. Above the piano in the vast lounge was a map where Mother kept track of the voyage, and I know she kept John's letters tied up in a silk ribbon on her bedside table.

~

In Britain, 1963 was even colder than the previous year, and the worst winter on record.

I was still riding to work looking like the Michelin Man, and this helped when I came off the Velo on an icy bend on route to Salisbury. I had the bizarre experience of sliding along spreadeagled on my back as I waved frantically at traffic coming the other way, then watching as my bike sailed by on its side and disappeared into a ditch.

Swathed as I was, I came to no harm except my dignity, and together with the news that our former bass player Wilkie had come off his Enfield on the Eastern Road and done a leg some real damage, the incident made me rethink my role as a motor bike boy. A day later I read in the *Portsmouth News* that my closest classmate from school had been killed in a head-on collision with a bus, and decided it was time for a change in personal transport.

~

It was all change on the national pop scene, and we had embraced home-grown heroes and heroines and hits.

Instead of the usual practice of copycatting American artists' chart successes, British singers and instrumental acts were doing it for themselves.

The UK charts were dominated by British compositions by British artists like Kathy Kirby, Billy J. Kramer, Billy Fury and, of course, the sensationally successful Beatles. The Shadows were riding high without Cliff, while former Shadows Jet Harris and Tony Meehan had hit the top of the charts with three records in a row.

From my perspective, all the new chart-busting bands like the Beatles had worked their way up from very small beginnings. This meant there was still hope for the Stormriders.

On the local scene, a handful of groups were making their mark, playing at big venues in Portsmouth and even going off the Island on tour. Unfortunately, the furthest away we had managed to get a gig was Gosport, and The Stormriders were still not causing much of a stir.

After much thought it occurred to me that perhaps I was too close to the action, and it was time to let someone else guide us to stardom.

~

Elvis had Colonel Parker, Tommy Steele, Billy Fury, Marty Wilde, Vince Eager, Terry Dene and Georgie Fame and Joe Brown raced from the stable of pop impresario Larry Parnes to chart-topping success.

Now, The Stormriders had acquired a Pompey coal merchant to propel us into the big time.

I don't remember how and where or when we were signed up by Jim Smith, but our first gig with him was certainly a change from our usual venues.

Since its heyday earlier in the century, The Theatre Royal was struggling to attract customers. One event which played to a packed house was the travelling wrestling circus, promoted by our new manager. Where once Marie Lloyd, Laurel and Hardy and perhaps even Charles Dickens had trod the boards, a ring would be set up and household names like Jackie Pallo, Mick McManus and Tibor Szakacs would go through their carefully scripted encounters.

Our job was to entertain the audience in between bouts. This meant dragging the amplifiers, drum kit, guitars and ourselves through the ropes and into the ring, then belting out a half-dozen songs. Because the audience had come to see their heroes draw blood, we were not a popular intermission, and apple cores, fish and chip wrappers and even bottles would fly as catcalls drowned out the music. It was not a promising start to our time in Gentleman Jim's hands, though we did collect a few full bottles of beer and the autographs of the most popular wrestlers.

~

It was a momentous decision, but I felt I had to move with the times, hair-wise.

I'd devoted six years and countless hours to perfecting my quiff, and had reckoned it rivalled the edifices of Cliff and even the King of Rock 'n' Roll for sleek shininess and rigid immobility. It had stood firm at a ton-up (100 miles an hour) on the back of a mate's motorbike, in rugby scrums and even the most energetic punch-ups. I had even reached the stage that with enough Amami Wave Set and blow-drying before a visit to the beach. I could dive in and then emerge with my hair still in place. It amazed people in the Snake Pit part of the beach in summer, and mothers had been known to bring their small children to see the phenomenon of the man rising from the waves with his quiff still standing.

Now, I felt that moving back to Southsea and to the big, posh house demanded a change of style and image. Elvis's quiff had never been the same since his Army days, and I reckoned Cliff and I were getting on a bit for such a teenage tonsorial tower.

So, it was goodbye quiff and hello Perry Como.

For those readers who are thinking 'Perry who?' Pierino 'Perry' Como was a very popular crooner of the Fifties and Sixties. His eternally memorable hits included *Magic Moments* and *Catch a Falling Star*. On the downside, one unforgettable offering consisted of fitting in the names of all the States, however tortuously. *Delaware* got its name from the punny refrain of 'What did Delaware?' followed by 'She wore a brand New Jersey', which was a bearable play on words. Almost unbearable was the query 'Why did California?' followed by the answer 'She called to say Hawaii 'Surprisingly (or not) the song was a huge hit and certainly did Perry's career no harm. Even though he was born in 1912 so unimaginably ancient to us young bloods, his neat, short flat-top hairstyle with a parting became the mode for millions of men at around this time. Teds stuck to their Ducks' Arses and older men to their savagely scraped-back Brylcreem-subdued centre partings, but for us trend-setters and fashion victims, a Como cut was where it was at. This would change, of course, when The Beatles mop-top fringes would take over the fashion world as well as the pop charts.

Blonde ambition: Mother and me jamming in the garden at St Edwards' Road

My poor old Velocette 350cc had gone, and my transformation from half-hearted Biker to toe-in-the-water Mod was complete. The so-called Mods and Rockers Wars on Brighton Seafront lay some years ahead, but the Mod subculture was becoming big time.

Starting in London, the fashion for riding around on noisy little Italian scooters was adopted by two sub-tribes. One set were the coolest of dandies, with three-button, tight Italian suits and slip-on loafer shoes or Chelsea boots with chisel toes. Their girls would echo their style with suit jackets and short but stylish haircuts. This masculine look contrasted intriguingly with lots of face and eye make-up, and the Pixie hairstyle and panda-eyed fashion icon of the mid-60s Twiggy typified the look.

The other sub-group were generally noisier in appearance and action. They went for fishtail parkas and more extravagant haircuts and sat astride Lambretta or Vespa scooters which were adorned with mirrors and long aerials with a fox's brush or flag at the top. Above all, the scooters had to stand out. I had a mate in the dockyard who made some real spending money by smuggling scooter side panels in to be dipped into a chrome bath.

The Mod fashion was influenced by a number of groups, typified by The Small Faces, The Jam and The Kinks. In 1973, The Who's rock opera *Quadrophenia* was the soundtrack for the retro-film of the same name about the Mod era. It brought about a brief revival of the fashion, but we were there first.

Ironically, the 'new' Mod style in the early Sixties of three-button Italian suit with narrow lapels and a handkerchief on prominent show was no different to what I'd been wearing since my first venture to Eastney Youth Club at 15. I was never much of a fashion-setter, but was to briefly become the talk of the Savoy for having a suit made without a collar. I had pinched the idea from Chubby Checker of *The Twist* fame and teen idol Bobby Rydell. It raised some eyebrows and was not to everyone's taste, but served an additional purpose as an opponent would not be able to grab the non-existent lapels to award me a Glasgow Header.

To go with my new image, I invested in a battered and barely roadworthy single cylinder 2-stroke Lambretta 124 that the previous owner had painted powder-blue.

With new flat-top hair, tight suit and shades, I was soon buzzing around Southsea with a French fag drooping from one corner of my mouth. It smoked itself but was anyway only there for show.

Unusually after several months, my band had the same name and line-up. But we had a new manager, and soon, a new outfit.

Topper (I never knew his name or where he lived) approached me at a regular gig at Hillside Youth Club. Paulsgrove and Wymering were districts on the northern fringe of the city, filled with council houses and, since the War, enclaves of quick-to-build 'prefabricated' homes, or as we unsurprisingly knew them, prefabs.

There was not a lot for young people to do on these bleak estates, and a number of them filled their leisure time with what we now call-anti-social behaviour. Hillside Youth Club was run by former boxer Ernie Littlefield and his wife Peggy to give youngsters somewhere to gather and expend their energy, and it thrives to this day.

We would alternate with other local groups, and always got a warm welcome. Once I remember it was a little over-warm when a critic threw a firework on stage, but there was no damage except to the thrower as he was ejected.

After the performance, Topper introduced himself and told us he was setting up a management company for stars of the future, and would like to represent us. He would find us fantastic venues and gigs as backing group to the likes of Billy Fury and The Beatles, but we would need to get up-to-date with our appearance.

As he pointed out, The Cadillacs, Mike Devon/ Beacon and the Diplomats and other more successful local bands all sported professional-looking stage outfits. Red or even tartan tuxedos with bow ties were popular. We were still wearing white shirts and more-or-less matching ties and looked, quite frankly, really amateur.

I took his point, collected the band members' measurements and called in to Shirt King, the go-to shop in Charlotte Street for Portsmouth followers of fashion.

The large, rotund and persuasive proprietor said he knew exactly what I was after. He said he had made stage suits for some of the top bands in the country, but didn't name any. We then went through a selection of materials and settled for a very shiny purple cloth with a sort of wood grain effect that reflected the light quite alarmingly. It looked suspiciously like curtain material to me, but Mr Shirt King assured me it was made for showbiz outfits, and just the right weight. It would, he said with an air of a man who knew what he was talking about, be very hot under the spotlights at the London Palladium.

I handed over the measurements and a deposit, and he said our 'suits of lights' would be ready in a fortnight.

It would be good to have a proper stage outfit, but a concern that we changed our line-up so often. Perhaps I would have to pick future replacements by their size rather than ability.

~

It was about now that, with a change of transport and hairstyle, I began my double life in earnest. But I didn't want to let go of my old life completely, and was still regularly meeting up with my mates at The White House, or what was to become our new local.

The Bridge Tavern in Somers Road was a bang-on Pompey boozer, run by Harry Atkins and his wife Brenda. It was Harry who had tried to bribe my band to take up residency in the rival pub across the road so he would benefit from the exodus of customers when we played. I took it as a gag but was never sure.

The Bridge was the new place to gather and discuss battle plans for the coming weekend. There was a great juke box, Harry and Brenda came from old Portsmouth families, knew the score and how to handle a pub-full of sometimes very dodgy characters.

A handful of girls had moved with us to our new HQ, but it was very much a man's place. The toilets were comfortably basic and apart from darts nights, catering was mostly limited to packets of crisps. You could, though ask for the Worcester sauce bottle to create what we called Vindaloo flavour.

Along with a few older locals, The Bridge was mostly frequented by some of the most well-known hard nuts in the city. As with the White House, there was never any trouble on the premises, as outsiders would not dare to come through the door, let alone start a ruck. Apart from our gang and immediate circle from White House days, frequent visitors included some well-known Pompey families and men-about-town like Big Ernie, Derek Polly, Mick Fenton, Georgie Peplow, Jackie Padley, Joey Newman, Les Dodds, Ginger Barber, Johnny Smith, Dave 'Budgie' Baron and his cousin Paul – who by now had just about spent his inheritance and lost his flash American car - and the two Charlies, Dobson and Saunders. An explosive pair, and one of them as we shall see later, quite literally.

~

In between going out on the town with The Boys and on gigs with the band, I'd assume my alter-ego and become a Southsea jet setter.

For a short while I tried an arty-farty goatee, but the boys at The Bridge Tavern, though accepting the loss of my quiff, would not stand for a bearded member of their gang.

I suppose some expert in psychology might say I moved between two worlds because I was myself neither one nor the other. My dad was a tough, working-class man from the Glaswegian Gorbals; my mother was or had been a proper lady before the family fortunes were lost in the Great Depression. I prefer to think I liked aspects of both social lifestyles, and having two sets of circles to move within gave me twice as much chance with girls from very different backgrounds. My double life got into full throttle when I adopted a set of white-collar mates and frequented the pubs and clubs my other circle would never use. It was not that I wanted to move on from the lads at The Bridge; I just wanted to experience other worlds and, with any luck, lots of top totty.

~

In both personas, my social life revolved mostly around a selection of public houses and meeting places.

A Friday night out with the Bad Boys from the Bridge Tavern would invariably kick off in the dodgy boozers in Commercial Road, and conclude at The Savoy Ballroom.

When out in company with the Posh Boys, the weekend outings would start in the hostelries of Kent Road, and conclude in the Pomme D'Or Club.

Built in 1847, the Portland Hotel was a formerly grandiose Grade II, clean-lined establishment in the centre of snobby Southsea. Over the years it went through a series of downward spirals and incarnations until going under the hammer in 2014, destined to live again as an upmarket apartment block.

Like an ageing beauty who is losing her looks, The Portland was getting shabby but still seen as an upmarket place to visit for a drink or meal. The manager was a very large, piratical-looking Welsh character named Lee Morgan. He had thick black hair, roseate cheeks, a ruddy snub nose and an enviable walrus moustache. He was a natural hotelier and licensee who knew his walk-in customers and catered for what they wanted.

The sumptuous lounge was all flock wallpaper and chintzy armchairs and sofas, and frequented by the gentlemen who flogged Rolls-Royces and Bentleys from the showrooms on the corner of my road. They shared a penchant for three-piece quality suits, RAF-style moustaches and a liking for large gin and tonics after work. Across the corridor was the domain of one of the most popular barmaids in the city.

Joyce Futcher was in her early middle age and born to be in the hospitality business. From behind the counter in Joyce's Bar, she would dispense drinks and sympathy or innocently flirt when needed. She had a raft of male customers who would stand almost shoulder-to-shoulder at the bar, and think that they were the only ones in Joyce's universe. She had them enslaved, even down to the gentle squeeze of the hand when she gave them their change.

Apart from the lonely fantasists, Joyce's Bar was favoured by members of the local tennis club and a diverse collection of single men who would become my Double Life set of friends. Mike and Mort were fairly senior Customs Officers. The athletic Morton had the look of a younger Yul Brynner, while Mike, with his lazy smile was so laid-back it was hard to tell if he had been drinking. Bob Symonds was of average height and fresh-faced, probably because of the ancient scooter he buzzed about the watering holes of Southsea on. He was a dapper young man who spoke as if rehearsing for a part in a P.G Woodhouse play, with talk of bimbling down the road and supping a swift half at the nearest hostelry.

Making up our circle was Pete Scott, who worked as an assistant in a naval tailor's shop in Queen Street. He was full of energy and mischievous wit, and like me, knew how to put on a front. He was decidedly one of the lads and from what we used to call a humble background, but when it suited, he spoke and acted like the poshest of his officer clientele.

After a couple of pints of Courage Director's Bitter when I was in my Dr Jekyll mode, our little group of men-about-town would set out from the Portland and take the short walk to Palmerston Road and Johnny Duthwaite's domain.

I never visited The Cambridge to find him absent, and Johnny D was truly a local legend in his own lifetime. He was a small, round man with a wise face who liked to work in a crisp white shirt with sleeves held up by silver armbands. His generously tailored trousers would be held up with wide braces to almost chest height. He was serenely calm at all times and floated around the three bars, nodding urbanely and sharing a few words with his best customers.

Unlike in many bars, the barmaids were attractive, immaculately dressed and of middle years. It was said that they were interviewed most rigorously by the landlord before being taken on.

Visitors could choose between a lofty-ceilinged large bar in post-Art Deco style or the thickly carpeted and more refined Smoking Lounge. It was said that Johnny never called time or rang a bell in all his years at The Cambridge, and eased customers off the premises by sheer force of personality.

Next stop on route to our club would be The Osborne, popular with the sort of customers who liked to be insulted in a mostly friendly way. Gordon the landlord was very good at knowing how far to go, and it was said that the more he liked you, the higher the level of insult. He must have liked me a lot.

~

Nowadays, pubs are more about food and décor and location than who holds the licence. In those days it was all about your host and how they attracted or repelled the punters. The final two pubs on our route to the Pomme were classic examples of the best in breed.

Tucked away in a road of interesting and upmarket terraced houses, The Auckland Arms was technically in the hands of Peter 'Salty' Salter. In actuality, it was known as Stevie's.

The Auckland claimed to be the smallest pub in Portsmouth, and the redoubtable Stevie more than filled it with her presence. She was a large, handsome woman, with a booming voice and unshockable nature. This was just as well. Stevie's day job was as proprietor of an upmarket one-stop bridal establishment in nearby Elm Grove. In the evenings, she would be on duty behind the bar of The Auckland. With her persona and her prince consort, the pub attracted a rich mix of what she called suited hooligans (me being a fine example), senior Naval officers and interesting types who would have been called bohemians or vagabonds in an earlier time. Any night might see talented local musician Jon Isherwood strumming his guitar in the back bar as a retired lieutenant, captain or even admiral told of past adventures in the Baltic when sneaky Jerry in his submarine was wreaking havoc with the convoys.

Moving on and just around the corner was the Apsley House. Though it naturally shared a number of regulars with the Auckland, they were two very different venues.

The Apsley was a rare Allied brewery 'foreign' pub in the Brickwood forest. The hosts were Max and Shirley, a patrician couple, and, unlike at the Auckland, were rarely seen on the working side of the bar counter.

The nearest I can come to describing the customer profile would be eclectic and the Apsley was very much a pub of two halves. There was a bar on each side of the entry passageway, and their doors led to different worlds.

I don't recall them being known as Public or Lounge, but they didn't need labels. The bar on the left had a linoleum floor, and came equipped with a football table and scrumpy cider. Across the passageway was all carpet and Regency wallpaper and the haunt of the Southsea *beau monde*, with a fair sprinkling of suited and unsuited hooligans.

Lined up on unofficially reserved stools might be Perry the high-class dentist, Pete 'Oh My Gawd' the Canadian lecturer in architecture, and lanky Peter Anderson, owner of an upmarket sports shop in

Elm Grove. Nearby would be a cluster of bank managers, solicitors and Chartered Accountants, talking shop and trying not to stare at the cleavage of the invariably remarkably endowed barmaids.

As in any gentleman's club, there were unspoken rules about mode of dress and behaviour, and even what place you occupied. I remember arriving one winter evening at a shade after opening time and standing at the bar alone as the barmaid busied herself preparing for the rush. A few minutes later, the door opened and a short, middle-aged man in a check suit strode in. Ignoring my nod of greeting, he marched to the fireplace, picked up a bottle of Guinness warming on the mantle-piece, then came to stand shoulder-to-shoulder with me. Though the bar was at least fifteen foot long and unoccupied, the little man pressed more and more forcefully against me. As he was small and old and I was sober and it was the Apsley, I shuffled sideways until the pressure eased. After fishing a bottle opener from his pocket, he smiled pleasantly at me and remarked what a clement evening it was. I realised then that I had broken the rules and been standing in his place.

In high summer, the bright young things who used the Pomme D'Or would gather outside the Apsley and watch the concourse of classy cars driven slowly past by the sons of ultra-rich businessmen. Soft-top MGs and Sunbeam Alpines would purr by as the young women looked on and probably made their choice of which car they would be going home in.

Like so many other pubs in those far-off days, the Apsley was a characterful pub, filled with characterful customers and run by characterful hosts. It existed in a time when people went to pubs to drink and talk and mix with their peers. Times change, and I do not think we will see their like again.

The New Me with Brother John at a posh wedding at The Queens Hotel. Note the thimble-sized sherry glasses and my sneaky weighing-up of a possible Top Totty conquest.

Like The Portland Hotel, the Auckland and Apsley House, the Pomme D'Or Club was a place that could only have existed at that time. It was in a basement, scruffy in a louche way, and the pretentious name suited the values of its members, even if many of them didn't know what it meant.

Along with naval officers (but never ratings) the core membership was young men and women with rich parents. On any night you could guarantee rubbing shoulders with the offspring of successful retailers, solicitors, accountants and long-established builders. And even a few now-respectable former crooks.

To maintain the image and snob-level, the owners made it near-impossible to gain entry if you were not of the right type. Visiting naval officers could take out a temporary membership on arrival at the basement door; it took me six months of pretending to be a distant relative of the Cadbury Family to become a member. Before then I had to ask a consenting adult to take me in, like a kid waiting outside a cinema showing an X-rated movie.

The Golden Apple was in the basement of a building at the end of what can fairly be claimed as a mews in Southsea, and the owners were Ted and Mrs Peacock. He was a large and affable chap with a tweedy jacket and neat moustache and the self-effacing air of a man under the matrimonial thumb. Mrs P was the dragon at the gate. You had to get past her to enter the dimly-lit premises.

Once in, it was prime totty territory for me. I would lie about my Sunbeam Alpine having broken down and sometimes persuade a lady member to walk to and admire the lights along the promenade from a convenient shelter. Best of all was when Mother and Father went off on a then-exotic skiing break and their flash pad on Portsdown Hill or the seafront became open house to all Pomme habitués. That was good news for me, but not so for the parents who came home to a cigarette-holed carpet in the lounge and a severely depleted wine cellar.

~

Back in the real world and at work I was still unhappy, but the job had got much more interesting and, because of that, bearable.

By now I'd mastered the mysteries of oxy-acetylene (gas) and arc (electric) welding, and it was rewarding to see the little pool of molten metal run neatly upwards, downhill or even horizontally at my command. It was even possible to recognise a welder's 'signature' by the size, shape and uniformity of the outer seam, and I made a point of making mine amongst the best.

As well as having my own mate to do the heavy and dirty work. I was getting more respect on-site and earning much better wages. But my double life was expensive, so I was glad when Mother said she had an idea that would give us both some spare cash.

I was not surprised that she would be looking for a new source of income. There was the rent from the garden flat, but Mother regarded that as unearned income, so not like the real thing. Although the snooker hall was doing well, now the boarding house in Castle Road and Kay's Store were in the past she needed to feel she was contributing to the family finances. I think the constant fear of losing everything came from when she was the youngest daughter of a family with two successful shops in Eastney. Then her grandfather made some unwise investments in the Depression of the late 20s and Mother had come home to find him with his head in the gas oven. She had had to leave school and go out to work, coincidentally in the corset factory on the corner of the road where she would later set up her convenience shop.

As Mother explained when she laid out her plans, she did not like to see our big garage being wasted on a parking space for dad's Alvis. With the boom in car-owning in mind, she had been looking in the *Portsmouth News* and seen how many second-hand cars were advertised for sale. She reckoned with shrewd buying and a minimum of attention, we could polish a few pounds into them. As she often said, you can sell anything at the right price; the trick was to buy it at the right price to make a profit.

Within a week, the new enterprise was under way, with a simple but winning formula. We would get the early edition of the News and pick a suitable car in an affordable range. Mother would then bargain the price down and I would spend a few evenings tarting it up. We stuck to Morris Minors, as they were reliable and popular. I would then paint the wheels, buff up the paintwork and repair or disguise any damage. I soon became an artist with a can of T-Cut scratch remover and dollops of the wondrous Isopon filler.

When I'd done my work, the car would be re-advertised in the paper and I would hide upstairs while Mother showed potential customers her beloved Maurice the Morris Minor. A natural saleswoman and actress, she played the innocent and while not lying, never revealed that the family car she was selling so regretfully had only been in the family for a week.

Kays Cars was terminated when we sold the only car we bought with a dodgy engine. Typically, the buyer said he needed Mrs East's nice little runner to travel long distances every day. Worse still, he added that he needed a reliable car as he lived in Basingstoke but worked at the Portsmouth tax office, specialising in looking into the affairs of small businesses trading in the City.

~

Near calamity and almost a loss to humanity.

The Lambretta was terminally injured and I had broken another window with my head. More seriously, I had torn the sleeve from and got blood all over my newest Italian suit.

Dawn was approaching and I had been on my way home from a visit to our former singer, Shaun Conlan. We had spent most of the night talking of old times and smoking and swallowing various substances, followed by a buzz along the seafront to wonder at the coloured lights and wave to the Kraken that he assured me was to be found dossing under the pier.

I had dropped Shaun off and nearly made it home before I forgot to take a corner and drove the scooter through the plate glass window of a shop somewhat ironically selling motor bike and scooter accessories.

As I lay quite contentedly amongst the wreckage and picked shards of glass from my fingers and face, the window of an apartment above a bank on the opposite corner opened and an elderly lady poked her head out.

She told me she had summoned an ambulance in case I needed it, and expected I would like a cup of tea. I agreed and after discussing the merits of Earl Grey as against English Breakfast, she arrived in a candlewick dressing gown, carrying a tray on which were two bone-china teacups and saucers, a plate of Dundee shortbread and a toilet roll.

She said she would keep me company till the ambulance arrived, and when I apologised for the noise waking her, she said she did not sleep much nowadays. She had lost her Army officer husband in the first War and been bombed out of her home on the seafront in the second. Life was quiet nowadays and it was interesting to meet new people, especially in unusual circumstances.

I agreed, and promised to come and see her for another nice cup of tea when my wounds had healed.

~

My next mode of transport was even more short-lived than my scooter.

Now I was a sophisticated man-about-town, it seemed to me that a car would better suit my image. It would also be much more suited to legover sessions in inclement weather.

In those pre-MOT days, a car was more or less deemed fit for the road if it had effective brakes and lights and a wheel in each corner, which at time of purchase my first motor car did.

With a fiver from an enthusiast restorer for my late Lambretta, I invested in a 1938 Morris Eight Tourer. It was that price because the doors on one side had been welded shut, and there was a sun roof in the form of a large hole above the driver's head. The headlining had long gone, but bearing in mind the intended use of the back seat and the current fashion for stiletto heels, I figured that would not last long anyway.

Sadly, the back seat was never tested.

I was driving a young lady to the Humps 'n' Bumps when I turned into the Ferry Road and felt a heavy lurch. I thought at first I had found a serious pothole, but the lurch was followed by a grinding sound and a shower of sparks appearing in the rear-view mirror, then we were overtaken by the offside rear wheel. Luckily, we were in the right place for an abandoned car, so I left it amongst the other detritus and walked my shaken date home, thinking of what might have been.

~

After a disagreement about the level of our payments (we would have liked some), we had lost our latest manager and I was back in charge.

I had already won us a new residency, and we would be playing regularly at the Court School of Dancing, next to Charlie Hurdle's pub in Eastney. It was a traditional gathering place for men in ill-fitting suits and women with a penchant for fluffy much-layered dresses and sequins. But, following George Turner at The Savoy's example, the manager had seen the need to adapt to modern times. Over the coming years, The Court would re-name and re-invent itself as many times as my band.

The Birdcage was a mod must, and staged some

big acts before they hit the big time. A friend has a poster advertising an early appearance of Long John Baldry, and, with bottom billing, a young man known as Rod 'The Mod' Stewart. Later it became a would-be cool cabaret club called The Pack, and then the trendy Cloud Nine. In the early years I remember Ginger Baker of the Cream falling from the stage as he was no longer able to hold his drumsticks due to intake of certain substances. Another time I was dragged into a mass brawl when Gary Farr (son of the acclaimed Welsh heavyweight champion boxer) and his band The T-Bones responded to unfavourable criticism from the floor. I remember Gary displayed a particularly stylish right cross.

All things pass, and nowadays, the site of all those memorable performances is a convenience store and petrol station.

Sic transit gloria mundi…

~

On the morning of our debut at The Court School of Dancing, I picked up our stage suits at Shirt King. The owner said they had turned out wonderfully well and would look particularly good on television with the way the material picked up the lights.

I still insisted on seeing them before paying the balance and, though they were certainly noticeable, could not help but notice they were missing several of the normal attachments or facilities associated with gentlemen's suits. When I pointed out that the jackets were unlined and would fit only where they touched, Mr Shirt King smiled at my ignorance and said the absence of lining and shoulder pads and other fripperies was deliberate because it would get very hot with our gyrating under TV and stage lighting.

When I remarked on the absence of pockets, he smiled and said that was normal for stage suits so as not to spoil the line if the artist thoughtlessly put anything in them. As to the lack of trouser zips, this was to avoid an embarrassing accident caused by forgetfulness. The waistbands were elasticised to make lowering them a matter of seconds. It would also make it easier, he said with a leer, to stuff a sock or two down the front and increase the appeal of our band to lady members of the audience.

The rest of the band was not so impressed with the curtain material outfits, but they were a hit with our lead singer.

Bert/Billy Storm was soon to be seen cycling round on his butcher's bike in his stage suit, and offered to wear a small sandwich board to further advertise the band.

~

The bookings were not getting any more frequent, but the Stormriders looked more like a proper band, and along with the stage suits we now had some state-of-the art kit.

To go with a pair of speakers which would fill the largest venue we were likely to play in, we now had what was believed to be the first portable echo chamber in the city. Previously, the only way to make your guitar and voice sound like they did on records was to sit in the toilet. Now the Watkins

Copycat had given bands the ability to recreate that studio sound. It was a small box containing a couple of heads and a loop of tape. It worked by recording voices and guitars and replaying them a fraction of a second later. With proper and modest use, the Copycat really did add to the sound value.

Unfortunately, and especially with drink or drugs taken, one of the band would always turn the dial to maximum echo. Together with our tendency to play in different keys when under the influence, not even the composer would have recognised our version of *Apache*.

~

It's said that everyone who was around at the time remembers exactly where they were when President John F. Kennedy was assassinated.

I certainly remember the moment I heard the shocking news, and it is stored in my memory as graphically as an old home-movie clip.

I was standing up in the bath, soaping my private parts in advance of a night on the town, when the door opened and my mother looked in. This was unusual enough, and before I protested, I saw her face was set in a grim expression. I could hear solemn music coming from the TV in the sitting room as she told me that President Kennedy had been shot and was dead.

The effect of the news on people around the world was truly remarkable. In Britain there was blanket coverage throughout the media for days, and tv and radio channels broadcast nothing but grim music and updates. Nowadays there might be a news flash if a world leader were to be assassinated, but I can't see the public putting up with missing out on the latest episodes of *Eastenders* or *Strictly Come Dancing.*

1964

~ Top of the Pops gets its first airing on BBCTV

~ Teenage girl's magazine Jackie is launched

~ The Beatles have their first number one in the US charts with *I Wanna Hold Your Hand*. This is to be the start of what is to become known as the British Invasion.

~ Later to become Muhammad Ali, Cassius Clay shocks the boxing world by defeating world heavyweight champion Sonny Liston

~ Richard Burton and Elizabeth Taylor marry for the first time

~ Britain and France agree a deal to construct a tunnel beneath the Channel

~ Radio Caroline becomes the first 'pirate' radio station in the UK, broadcast from a ship anchored off the east coast

~ The Beatles make the unprecedented achievement of taking the top five spots in the US Billboard charts

~ The twelve 'Great Train Robbers' are sentenced to a total of 307 years

~ Nelson Mandela is sentenced to life imprisonment in South Africa

~ The last judicial hanging in the United Kingdom takes place in Liverpool

~ The Kinks release their first album

~ The Labour party wins the General Election ending thirteen years of Conservative rule. The new Prime Minister is Harold Wilson
~ The first Beatles' film, *Hard Day's Night* is released
~ Dr Martin Luther King Jnr. is awarded the Nobel Peace Prize

Top Brit Tunes

Hippy, Hippy Shake ~ The Swinging Bluejeans
Swinging on a Star ~ Big Dee Irwin with Little Eva
Stay ~ The Hollies
Diane ~ The Bachelors
5-4-3-2-1 ~ Manfred Mann
Not Fade Away ~ The Rolling Stones
Can't Buy Me Love ~ The Beatles
A World Without Love ~ Peter and Gordon
The Rise and Fall of Fingel Blunt ~ The Shadows
Hold Me ~ P J Proby
The House of the Rising Sun ~ The Animals
It's Only Make Believe ~ Billy Fury
Have I The Right? ~ The Honeycombs
As Tears Go By ~ Marianne Faithfull
You Really Got Me ~ The Kinks
He's in Town ~ The Rocking Berries
Doo Wah Diddy ~ Manfred Mann
Um, Um, Um, Um, Um, Um ~ Wayne Fontana and
the Mindbenders

Walking through the park, it wasn't quite dark
There was a man sitting on a bench
Out of the crowd as his head lowly bowed
He just moaned and he made no sense
He'd just go
Um, um, um, um, um, um
Um, um, um, um, um, um
Um, um, um, um, um, um
Um, um, um, um, um, um

Um, Um, Um, Um, Um, Um - performed by Wayne Fontana and the Mindbenders with lyrics by Curtis Mayfield

As the new year dawned, two thoughts occurred to me. One that I was about to leave teenagerhood behind, and the other was that in less than twelve months I would be released from the requirements and restraints of my apprenticeship. Soon, I would be free to make the next steps on my journey through life. All I had to do was work out where I wanted those steps to take me. A no-brainer was that anywhere away from building sites and towards fame and fortune would suit me nicely.

Escaping from Brightside would offer many options, including travel to faraway places to find myself. It was not that I was particularly lost; I just didn't have a clue as to what I wanted to do, apart from becoming extremely rich and famous.

The lack of real progress for the band was frustrating; if we were still treading water by the end of the year, I might realise my ambition of renting a garret in Paris and turning my hand to becoming a famous painter. The time of *zinc* bars and pouring the Green Fairy (absinthe) over a sugar cube while talking through the night about Life and Art were long past, but I figured that with the trend for throwing tins of paint at a canvas my lack of experience and talent would not necessarily be a barrier to success.

Or, more sensibly, I might follow in my brother's wake and bluff my way onto a ship as an engineer. Rather than a tramp steamer, I figured I would prefer a cruise liner, where I might cut a dash in my uniform and take the fancy of a rich and beautiful heiress. Or even a not so beautiful but still rich older widow.

Or, if I could save some money, I might have a crack at hitchhiking my way around the globe to see what life was like in other, distant places. I'd always been curious about how they did things in foreign lands, or even outside the boundaries of Portsea Island. My first attempt to break free had come at five years of age, when I left my mother's side unnoticed and stowed away on a boat at the quayside in Old Portsmouth.

I was quickly found by a deckhand and sent back to where Mother was waiting anxiously. The journey did not take long as I had chosen the Gosport ferry for my means of escape to distant lands.

Now, in less than a twelvemonth I would be free to go and do what I wanted; rather than euphoria, the thought brought a sense of uncertainty and even fear.

~

Another posting, and this one would allow me to casually drop into conversation at the Pomme D'Or that I'd been to Charterhouse public school.

This was technically true, as I was to spend several months at that most exclusive seat of learning to sort out their ancient and dodgy heating system.

I had not previously thought of myself as a resentful or bitter type, but after throwing away my academic chances, it hurt and angered me to see true privilege at work. I would be cursing and struggling with a heavy length of pipe in the boiler house, and look out on groups of boys not much younger than me, strolling across the ancient quadrangle with an assured step. On my knees at a manhole cover, I would hear Latin phrases floating from open windows, or watch the members of the rugby team jogging to the playing fields. Watching, I would imagine what it would have been like to have been born to such a life. Then I would pull myself together and think how lucky I was in many other ways and how much sweeter fame and fortune would taste when I had earned it.

Looking back, it is curious how I always believed it was only a matter of time before I made it to the big time. More than forty years ago I thought I'd done it when I wrote a book about a schoolboy with magical powers who takes on Evil and triumphs. Twenty-seven publishers said thanks but no thanks, then along came Harry Potter. As they say, that's how the cookie crumbles, and I'm not bitter. Much.

~

While talking about the daily slog of bus and train marathons for the round trip of a hundred miles from Portsmouth to Godalming, Mother suggested it was time I should buy another car.

She was right and it was true that I'd recently passed the driving test on the second attempt. After the first examiner failed me with what seemed unseemly relish, I found out he was a recently retired City policeman. I suspected he might have given me the thumbs down because of my brushes with his former colleagues and put it to him before I left the car. He had smiled quietly and assured me it was not through prejudice that I had failed the test, but for driving too fast and too carelessly, and for using the rear-view mirror to look at myself rather than the road behind.

When I reminded Mother that I had not repaid her loan to buy the long-dead Velocette, she said she still owed me my share of the profits from the short-lived Kay's Cars. Ever one to spot an opportunity, she pointed out I could give my carless workmates a lift, charge them half the railway fare and still make a handsome profit.

~

I think most people keep a special place in their hearts and memories for their first car. I didn't have time to get to know and love the wheel-shedding Morris, and prefer to think of the Austin as my first proper motor. This may also be because it was the first one that was taxed and insured and that I had a licence to drive.

Unlike my boxy Morris and other pre-war cars, the

1953 Somerset A40 was a nicely rounded saloon with what the designers called 'transatlantic style' curves instead of corners. When new, it had boasted a top speed of 74 mph and that it would get there in a matter of minutes. Given that there are sixty minutes to the average hour, this was a safe claim.

The A40 also boasted all the modern accessories, like two wing mirrors and proper, inbuilt flashing direction indicators. Other significant improvements on the old Ford were that there were no significant holes in the bodywork and all four doors were fully operational. Even more impressive, the front seats were covered with real leather, which gave off that incomparable, rich bouquet when the sun shone. Being nearly a decade old, my new car had none of the modern luxuries like a radio or heater, and the windscreen wipers worked only when you talked to them nicely. On the coldest of January mornings, my front seat passenger would have to scrape the ice off the inside of the windscreen with a coin so I could see where we were going.

When in Mr Hyde mode, the Somerset was invaluable as what we then called a passion wagon, and the headlining above the back seat was soon torn by gyrating stiletto heels. On a night out with the boys, it would accommodate five at a squeeze. There was no limit to how much you could drink and get behind the wheel, and the only offence was to drive when your ability was '...for the time being impaired by alcohol'.

As well as tragic for those who lost dear ones because of drink-related accidents, it must have been very frustrating for traffic duty police officers.

I know it used to drive our arch-nemesis PC Jennings into a fury when he pulled me over to no effect. He was a narrow-faced and mean-moustached man who rode on a water-cooled Velocette with leg shields like cricket pads. They were known by us as 'Noddy bikes' and I think the almost contemptuous attitude fuelled his antagonism towards all young road users. He would regularly pull me over when we'd been on a pub crawl, and the smell of five men full of beer must have been overwhelming when he ordered me out of the car to perform a sobriety test. This would involve me touching the tip of my nose, counting my fingers, and walking along the kerb in a straight line. No matter how many pints I'd sunk, being pulled over always had a sobering affect and he never got me. I'm not proud of my days of drinking and driving, and thank my lucky stars I never had an accident or hurt anyone during the hundreds of times I drove with a gallon of beer under my belt.

In Dr Jekyll mode, I'd take pains not to be seen at the wheel of the A40 by anyone of my posh set from the Pomme D'Or Club. On the odd occasion I was spotted, I'd explain that I'd been driving the old banger to Harry Pounds's scrap yard as a favour to an aged and impoverished friend. To further aid deception, I had an Austin-Healey 3000 Sports key fob to toss on the bar while ordering up a pink gin.

~

To the joy of our parents, brother John had returned home safely from the sea after his circumnavigation of the planet in a tramp steamer.

He was deeply bronzed and achingly good looking and dashing in the uniform he wore when Mother opened the door. Like me he was one for making an appearance. Also like me, he had adopted a new persona, although his metamorphosis was permanent.

To my joy I was gifted almost his entire wardrobe as he equipped himself with hacking jackets, cavalry twill trousers and even a check flat cap. He now routinely dressed as if on his way to a point-to-point meeting.

Having come back with a big stash of cash - he said it was hard to spend much while steaming up the Limpopo River - he announced he was going to become a purveyor of 'cherished' motor cars. As he had inherited a combination of Mother's business acumen and dad's amiability and good fellow-ness, it was generally agreed he would do well flogging used cars to the wives of the local gentry.

Needless to say, as a former Merchant Navy officer and up and coming member of what passed as the Portsmouth Jet Set, he was nominated, seconded and awarded membership of the Pomme D'Or within a week. I had joined looking for posh totty; John joined to build up a network of new and influential friends. Once he had counted the fearsome Harding brothers and other Pompey hard nuts as fighting friends; now he hobnobbed with the sons of the very rich and slept with their daughters.

To suit his new image, he had invested in a vintage Morgan sports car in British Racing Green and complete with the wide leather belt over the bonnet.

Mooching round in his room for any unconsidered

trifles he would no longer value, I found a business card which showed the transformation was complete. He had now taken Mother's maiden name and the name above our posh address was John Pitt-East. I was still switching uncertainly from one persona to another; John had made the change for good and left his past and name behind.

~

After a Saturday evening gig on Clarence Pier, I found myself with a further change to the location and shape of my nose.

The boys from the band had taken the kit and themselves home in an old van we'd clubbed together and bought, and I'd chosen to walk across Southsea Common to the Pomme D'Or Club for a late-night trawl.

I don't know why the two figures who loomed out of the darkness chose to set about me. It couldn't have been a mugging as they didn't go through my pockets as I lay on the ground. Though it was dark, my haircut made it unlikely to have been a pair of lads indulging in the weekend sport of sailor-bashing. It might have been a possessive boyfriend with help, a score to be settled or even a pair of music-lovers who'd been to the gig on the pier.

For whatever reason, they had made a good job of working me over, and it still rankles that I will never know who they were and why they attacked me. Funny how, even if you never get payback, it helps if you know who gave you a beating, and why. Especially if you deserved it.

~

As recalled earlier, it's said that everyone who was around at the time remembers where they were and what they were doing when President Kennedy was assassinated. Another year on and another totally unexpected event is engraved in my memory. Along with a deep regret I did not follow my convictions about it.

I heard about the killing of Kennedy when standing in the bath. I was sitting in the toilet having a bowel motion when I heard that Cassius Clay had beaten Sonny Liston to become the new world heavyweight boxing champion.

It was such a shock because all the big money had been on Liston, who had criminal convictions and the look of a stone-cold killer. Our own Henry Cooper's manager has refused to put him in the ring with Liston, and said he would not even want to meet him walking down the street. At 22, Clay was a Golden Globe winner and known as the 'Louisville Lip 'because of his outrageous pronouncements. A doctor who examined Clay before the bout said he was like a man frightened to death, and the scene was set for a crushing defeat.

To everyone's surprise except mine, Clay won. It was one of the only two occasions I can remember being absolutely certain of an outcome that went against expert opinion and even common sense.

Brother John and dad had stayed up all night to hear the fight on the radio, and John shouted the news through the toilet door as he passed. What really hurt was that I had actually accumulated a few quid from a series of all-night 'ghoster' shifts and had £37 in notes and change wasting its time in the fruit bowl on my bedside table. As my dad had said, the odds against Clay winning were an unheard of 8-1 for a two-horse race, but neither he and John had a bet because the outcome was so obvious.

In spite of my conviction, I chickened out and spent months afterwards regretting my lack of nerve. Had I put all my spare cash on Clay, the winnings would have bought a not-too used Austin Healey 3000 to match the fake fob which held the keys of my old Austin Somerset.

Cassius Clay went on to become Muhammad Ali and, in my opinion, one of the greatest sportsmen and human beings who ever lived.

In case you're wondering, the only other time I remember being absolutely certain of an outcome was when I met a very pretty and tolerant friend-of-a-friend and knew we would be together forever. Or as long as we both might live.

~

Looking like a cut-price Man in The Iron Mask, I was relaxing on a grassy knoll, looking out at the rolling Wiltshire countryside and snacking on a Curly-Wurly. Laying by my side, a visiting lady friend was generously giving me what was known in the profession as 'hand relief.' If this was a typical example of post-op treatment, I was all for it.

~

Odstock hospital was built in 1942 to treat badly injured American soldiers, and in the post-war years had become known for its specialist burns unit and pioneering work in skin-grafting.

Star of many a hit TV show and then adored charity champion Jimmy Savile had done much good there, and probably much bad. We met briefly during my stay, when he asked why I was there. I explained it was to have my nose put back in shape, to which he responded anything would be better than what I had now.

When I had seen my doctor in the hope he would be able to fix it, he had said the damage was more than he could handle. I would suffer badly with sinus problems in later years if something was not done so I could start breathing through it again as Nature had intended. He had sent me to see a specialist, and the result was that I was invited to be, if not a guinea-pig, a practice pad. In simple terms, instead of trying to knock it back into shape, the plan was to take out the old bone and replace it with a bit off the end of one of my ribs. It was a fairly new procedure, but the odds were in my favour.

If I had been concerned with what was to come, I realised when I arrived how relatively trivial and pain-free my treatment would be.

In the next bed was a young man strung up by his head, arms and heels from a metal goalpost. I tried not to wince at the smell of corruption, and saw that the remains of his right foot had been stitched to a bloody flap cut from but still attached to his left calf. Though obviously heavily sedated he was conscious and even raised a smile as our eyes met. After he had apologised for the smell, we introduced ourselves and Terry explained that he had thoughtlessly shot half his foot away while out at night keeping the local rabbit population in check.

The idea was to try to get the lump of flesh from his calf to agree to live with the leftovers of his foot. When it did, they would detach the flap from his calf and carve and stitch it to make the approximation of a foot shape. So far and as I could see and smell, the two bits of him had refused to become one.

Over the next week, the brave Terry and I became friends. The nurses would look after the specialist stuff with bed pans and bottom wiping, and I would put cigarettes in his mouth, feed him snacks, read to him and scratch, within reason, wherever he had an itch.

By the end of the week, I'd been wheeled into the theatre and had, as the surgeon explained, my nose bone broken with a shiny stainless-steel hammer, extracted and thrown into the waste bin. After sawing a small piece off the bottom rib on my right side, he had hammered it in place and done some neat stitchwork.

For the next week I had two very black eyes, a sore side and the results of the operation hidden behind a metal guard. When it came off, my new nose was as straight as that on the bust of a Roman Emperor. After an early snub and later flattened nose, it looked somehow alien and unfitting to me, and my visiting hand maiden agreed. She said it made me look poncey and asked if it could not be put back as it was.

As it happened, she got her wish. On my first night out after returning home, I took it and myself to The Bridge Tavern to show it off. One of the boys known to have quick hands aimed a Karate chop at it, intending to stop the blow an inch before making contact. It was his party trick, but after three pints of scrumpy, his timing was a little off.

I now had a newly broken nose, and I took it as a signal that Fate never intended me to look like a Roman emperor, more perhaps a Roman pugilist who was not too good at defending himself in the arena.

~

On the Dark Side of my social life, I'd mostly kept out of trouble and not picked up any further criminal convictions. But I did come close when playing a popular if thoughtless after-chucking-out-time game one too many times.

The activity involved running out of Indian restaurants without paying. I make no excuses except that it was done without a thought of the legal or moral perspectives. How thoughtless we were is shown by the way we sometimes ran before the meal arrived, and sometimes before we even ordered. In any case, it was a short-lived fashion and turned out to be an expensive indulgence for me.

The Green Mask in Southsea was our restaurant of choice to bump, mostly because the toilet window gave access to an asbestos-roofed outhouse which we could scramble across and from there drop into a side road. We liked the owner and particularly his Chicken Phal, so we would always pay for the previous meal when we arrived for the next one. I suspect the owner added a surcharge to cover any inconvenience as, although he knew what was coming, he would always seat us at the table closest to the toilet door, and even apologise if it were occupied.

Our Friday night chicken phal run came to an end when I put a foot through the asbestos roof and left half my trousers behind, then spoiled the jacket when I fell amongst the bins in the side road.

~

We might be having less punch-ups with members of the audience at Stormrider gigs, but were making up for it by scrapping amongst ourselves. Sometimes it was just verbal, but at times blows were thrown. Sometimes an outbreak of in-fighting anticipated The Who's penchant for smashing up their instruments; the difference was that we couldn't afford the replacement cost. We also lost a guest singer who was almost as out of it as us at a gig, and flung himself off the stage to crowd surf without noticing there was no crowd to break his fall.

I was beginning to see that there was no future for a band that had had more members than the average audience, constantly fell out and often played in different keys.

Then came what could be our big break.

Along with other local groups we had acted as back-up to some big names when they appeared at The Savoy. The more successful bands got the choicest bookings, and our old singer Mike Beacon and his new group The Diplomats were the supporting act for the Beatle's historic appearance. The story went that the legendary manager George Turner had booked them before they had hit the big time with *From Me To You*. Moreover, he had got them for just £50, a snip even all those years ago.

The Stormriders had been a support act for

Chris *Let's Dance* Montez and Cliff *Sounds like Locomotion* Bennett and the Rebel Rousers but now we had a chance to win a national competition to find the Best of British music acts. It was run by the Butlin empire and the Southern Central Heats were taking place at The Savoy at the end of the month. I'd sent a recording of *Be-Bop-a-Lula* made at Hillside youth club. To our delight, we were awarded a place in a regional heat and I made a note to have our suits of lights laundered, our instruments cleaned and tuned properly, and to ban any attempts at crowd-surfing or the taking of any pills of any colour before or during our big break.

I also had to hope that the judges on the night had not heard the cassette tape, or they would be sure to realise that I had sent in a recording of another, far more accomplished local band.

~

Another summer and another persona to adopt in my struggle to find myself, or at least what and who might be the real me.

I'd already posed as a half-hearted Teddy Boy, uncommitted Biker, moderate Mod, middle-class young man-about-town, would-be local rock hero and punch-up specialist. The truth was that I never felt much enthusiasm for any of my guises, or I'd have gotten more into them. My biker mates had become ever more committed to seriously injuring or killing themselves while roaring about on superbikes and meeting at caffs to earnestly discuss torque ratios and the merits of the BSA Gold Star and the Norton Manx Special. My short-lived Mod incarnation had ended when the old Lambretta scooter crashed through the shop window after a night on the weed. Even my posturing as a local impresario and competent guitarist and vocalist was a fake. All the other Pompey bands seemed to be doing better than mine: The Stormriders were getting nowhere and I couldn't carry a tune and even after all the gigs and practice sessions, I relied on no more than four chords. The only thing I seemed consistently good at and fond of was drinking and fighting and shagging, and those qualifications didn't seem to offer much of a future. I couldn't think of a job where I would be paid to drink or brawl, and wasn't physically equipped to become a big-name porn movie star. Then I had a summer dalliance with an art student, and my inner chameleon went into overdrive.

Jazz was in her final year at the Portsmouth College of Art, and not at all the sort of girl I would normally pay court to. She was tall and lean with dirty fingernails, a flat chest, a manner as spikey as her hair and more tattoos than little Ginger Barber, the Pompey Illustrated Man. We met in a coffee bar under an archway in Portsea when she asked me what the fuck I was looking at. I told her it was the tattoo of Andy Warhol's chicken noodle soup can on her forearm, and she offered to show me the Vermeer on her back if I let her sketch me wearing nothing but my socks in Victoria Park.

I agreed, and so began my brief career as a fake student. It was actually the most poignant of times, as it seemed to confirm how much more suited I was to a Bohemian, artistic lifestyle than welding pipes together for a living. So, I would I decided, try being a part-time hippy.

~

After teddy boys and mods and rockers, a new lifestyle trend had crossed the Atlantic and reached Portsmouth via London. History records it as a 'counter-culture', starting in the mid-60s and identified generally as the Underground Movement. From what I could see, most of the groups were less interested in bringing the government down as in having a good time and getting out of their heads on the go-to drugs of the time. The sub-culture had its own music and bands like The Velvet Underground (led by Lou 'Walk on the Wild Side' Reed) and Hawkwind and later, Pink Floyd. The movement had its own magazine, The International Times, and even its own language, though hearing someone saying 'Yeah Man', 'cool' and 'right on' in a Pompey accent never worked for me. Unlike previous sub-cultures of trends, there were no fixed dress rules or style except generally scruffy in a 'we don't care about fashion', fashion. The men would go for unkempt mop-top hair, sleeveless fleece jackets and tattered jeans. Women would go for long, straight hair, pale lipstick, white faces and panda eyes. Both sexes might wear a beaded headband, with or without a feather. Think Sonny and Cher and you will get the picture. They were anti-war and anti-authority, and some would say anti-personal hygiene. Liberal application of pachouli oil was very popular with both sexes, as the strong odour not only covered the smell of stale sweat but also the bouquet of marijuana. The members of this loose affiliation of like minds were known as Hippies, Beatniks or by a lot of Pompey people, Dirty Smelly Bastards. The common link seemed to be an unworkable philosophy and solution to the world's problems, pretentious music and lots of drugs.

In Portsmouth there were a handful of brave hippies who would venture out in public in daylight, and being Portsmouth, the movement mostly developed into a student sub-sub-culture. The proponents would gather in smoky rooms above pubs or dimly-lit former church halls to drink cheap booze, take drugs and dance to traditional or sometimes modern jazz. Standard dress could include a really baggy sweater, often reaching to the knees and tight black jeans with optional paint stains. Footwear was optional, and I once saw a man who looked remarkably like comic Tony Hancock and who appeared to be wearing winkle pickers with immensely long and pointed toes. When I looked closer, I saw that he had rolled sheets of cardboard into cones and taped them on to a pair of standard shoes. He was dancing what was called the Bunny Hop, a gentler forerunner of punk pogo-ing, but his partner kept landing on and squashing his winklepicker points.

Jazz (I never knew her real name) and I lasted a glorious two months, drinking scrumpy and smoking dope, skinny dipping and having energetic fucks (she refused to call it 'making love') on the beach. In between we'd camp at music festivals, and frequented the Swing G club. This was a weekly gathering of jazz fans held in various pubs, and run by my old school mate, bow-tie and trumpet aficionado, George Langton.

Enthused by free form modern jazz and how easy it sounded to be making it up as you went along, I thought I might do better at making a tune with my mouth than my fingers, so bought a second-hand tenor saxophone. I had six lessons before the owner of the shop told me he had never known anyone so unable to get anything resembling a note from any musical instrument, and offered to buy it back from me at more than the price I had paid for it.

~

Jazz had moved on, and I'd returned to my Jekyll and Hyde duo of personas.

Thanks to my encounter with the asbestos roof at the Green Mask my trendy Italian three-piece was now legless as well as collar-less. It was time for a change, and one to suit my double life.

For the past year, the design components of my suits were as curious a mix as my social life. In a nod to Mod fashion, I had opted for tight-fitting, four-buttoned jackets. As an echo of my half-hearted teddy boy semi-drape days, the jacket would be lined with an eye-catchingly shiny shade of Kingfisher Blue or Aztec Gold. In a gesture towards to my Portsmouth pop band impresario status, I had, as previously mentioned, dispensed with lapels after seeing a collarless coat modelled by Bobby Rydell*. I now had a selection of classy cast-offs from brother John, but decided to splash out on a quality three-piece, made by a local 'bespoke' tailor.

I would also need another suit for when I was in Hyde mode.

The speedily-made whistle and flute was not a problem. The one to wear when hob-knobbing with the Southsea jet-set needed to be really classy and show in a restrained way that it was a pricey one.

After asking round in the Pomme, I found my new tailor in Albert Road, a door or two from the King's Theatre.

Mr Stanley had a round-faced, snub-nosed Polish face and an unpronounceable first name. He also had a halo of wispy fair hair and a most cheerful countenance. He smiled throughout my first fitting, and that may have been because of the design I insisted on, or the prospect of how much he was going to charge me for all the whistles and bells.

Adding to the singularity of the shop and its proprietor, Mr Stanley's assistant was what we in those un-PC days called a dwarf or midget. Dennis had a puckish face and waspish sense of humour, and when he took my measurements, he made a joke about it being easier for him to take an inside leg length because he could do it standing up. What it must have been like for him to run a tape measure over someone without a deformed spine and fore-shortened limbs I cannot imagine, but he never showed an ounce of self-pity at how cruel the casual hand of Fate could be.

Pop nerd factette: Bobby Rydell was a teen idol most remembered for his 1960 hit 'Wild One'. As a sly insider reference, the school in the film of the musical 'Grease' was named Rydell High.

~

After an initial consultation and some discreet eyebrow-raising at some of my instructions, Mr Stanley told me to come back in a week for a first fitting. He also told me the price, which made me weak at the knees. But, I told myself, I must expect to pay the going rate if I wanted to look like the sort of person James Bond would ask for sartorial advice.

It's hard to over-emphasise the impact the Bond movies had on the style and culture of the mid-Sixties. *Goldfinger* was the third 007 movie and a huge international box office success. The sardonic hero not only appealed to women, but it was said all men wanted to be him. Judging by the way they acted on leaving the cinema, that was a fair comment.

I remember coming out of the Essoldo in Southsea after Bond had foiled the villain and scored with Pussy Galore, then realising I had narrowed my eyes and was slinking down the road as if on constant alert for danger from an agent of SMERSH. Then I realised that the other men leaving the cinema were also acting and walking with their interpretation of a Bond gait, some with a hand inside their jacket as if keeping a cautious hold on their Walther PPK pistol.

~

I never knew his name or what he did for a living, but my local role model and inspiration for the new suit frequented the casino in Southsea's poshest hotel.

Like the Portland, The Queen's was a magnificent

building which had seen better days, and was now owned by the legendary Billy Manning, owner of Southsea fun fair. It was said he bought it to put a finger up to the local gentry, and would sit in his giant trailer at the fair ground, looking across the Common with a smile of satisfaction.

Later to become part of the Playboy Club next door in Kimbell's Ballroom, the casino was on the first floor in the Queen's and the baroque splendour was a perfect Bondian setting.

It was common for non-gamblers to drop in to savour the sophisticated atmosphere and see and be seen, and my hero was invariably there, sitting at the roulette table with a hand-made Balkan Sobranie cigarette dangling from one corner of his mouth. For all I know, he was called Bert Ponsonby and worked for the Post Office, but to me he was 007 incarnate.

He would sit, head on one side as he regarded the table and players with a casual but observant eye, occasionally taking a sip from his glass of what I imagined must have been a superior brand of single malt whisky.

I don't know if he was actually playing at being James Bond, but he was tall and dark and wore the same half-amused expression as he looked around. I couldn't look like him, but I reckoned I could have a suit based on his.

It looked like it was some sort of gaberdine, with long, narrow and rolled lapels. It had two buttons at the front and a single vent at the back. Most importantly, the buttons at the cuff actually worked, rather than - like my Jackson suits - being just for show. My hero always left the first one undone, probably to make sure people knew they were the real thing.

~

My new Mr Hyde suit was ready in a couple of weeks. The Dr Jekyll/James Bond three-piece with real cuff buttons took more than a month of fitting and tweaking before Mr Stanley announced he was satisfied.

At last, I stood in front of the cheval mirror, admiring myself and adopting my version of the narrow-eyed Bond look. I was working on raising one eyebrow when my new bespoke tailor asked me if there was a problem, and did I need to borrow his spectacles. I said it was just a touch of migraine, but I'd also noticed he had not fitted the red lining or several other design features I'd asked for. It was his turn to wince, and he said he had used the charcoal grey lining as his supplier had run out of Burgundy Red. He must have forgotten what he called the other 'elements', or they had been lost in translation. His English was not good, and for the oversight he must blame his assistant. Dennis looked suitably chastened, and after I changed back into my box jacket and jeans ensemble, Mr Stanley handed me the bag containing my new suit. With it was an envelope which contained what he called his account. He would appreciate early settlement, he added. As his assistant opened the door with a flourish, he said that with care the suit would last for many years, and reminded me before I looked at the bill that quality never came cheap.

~

The new suit was working, and my little black book was filling up fast with double-barrelled and familiar names. I was interested to find that the origins of the term came from the time when rulers - including- Henry VIII - would literally keep a black book listing all those who had done them a disservice or were for other reasons not in favour. Much later, the term came to be associated with the habit of bachelors keeping a register of names and phone numbers of available female companions.

Sad and such an obvious sign of inadequacy that it now seems, I had a notebook with a black cover in which I kept a record of all my sexual conquests. The entries registered where and with whom I had, as it were made an entry, and how much I had enjoyed it. A typical entry in the book might read: *October 19, Penny Hassett-Smythe, shelter by the War Memorial, knee-trembler. 7/10.* I never heard of one of the Pomme girls keeping a record of their amorous adventures, but I'm sure they must have talked about mutual lovers and their performances. I'm just glad I never heard any verdicts on my performance.

~

By day I was wearing a set of smelly overalls while welding giant pipes together at Fawley oil refinery; by night I was wearing either my Mr Hyde or Dr Jekyll suit while moving in between two very different worlds. It was an expensive pair of life- styles to maintain, and at weekends I was earning some extra what he called my crumpet money by helping out at brother John's new business. He had unsurprisingly turned out to be a natural car dealer, and success had meant he now had a proper showroom rather than our garage and a stretch of kerb outside the front door at St Edwards Road.

With the remains of his savings from the round the world trip, John had bought a small yard and showroom in Southsea. Austin Autos. I would help out by cleaning stock and driving cars to the weekly Southampton Auctions. There, we would meet up with members of the Portsmouth brotherhood of used car salesmen. In those days few people would have the confidence to buy and sell cars for a living or even a side-line, so the brotherhood was a small and select bunch.

It was almost as much of a social as a business event, and tall tales would be told over bacon sandwiches and Bovril from the van by the auction yard. Pleasantries over, the members would stroll around the cars to go under the hammer, making a note not to bid on any of the lots fancied by one of the ring. I learned how to spot cars which had been 'clocked' and claimed a far lower mileage than they had done. Also, fairly common practices like sawdust or even bananas to mask ugly transmission sounds or porage oats in the oil. Holes in the bodywork were regularly filled with a mix of filler and mashed-up cigarette packets.

Brother John was above these practices, and sometimes the victim of people who hired cars and didn't bring them back. That earned me some extra pocket money when John and I would go and reclaim the vehicle, leaving a painful reminder to the customer that crime does not always pay.

By far my favourite perk was to take my brother's

powder-blue 1962 Jaguar E-type for its weekly wash and refuelling. Although the petrol station was only a mile away, I would spend at least an hour tooling along the seafront road with my shades on and a casual arm resting on the window ledge, hoping to be seen by any fanciable females or members of the Pomme D'Or. It was an expensive ruse, because, as well as having to invest in a Jaguar key ring for use in the clubs and bars, just cruising along the esplanade for an hour would use up at least two gallons.

~

As our date with destiny at the Savoy approached, I summoned a meeting of the band for a serious talk about the talent contest. After a long talk on what number we should perform, we decided to go with *Whole Lotta Shakin'*. This was because it was a quite dramatically theatrical number, could be stretched or shortened to any length, and any discords or in my case dischords would not be so noticeable.

I also had a serious talk with the boys about abstaining from uppers and downers on the night of the performance, and hopefully for the weeks leading up to it.

~

A couple of hours after lecturing the band about not indulging in toxic substances, I was under the influence of a sugar cube.

It came from the fridge of former Hot Rod lead guitarist and close friend, Tony Nabarro. I'd dropped into his flat in Southsea, and he asked me if I had tried the latest green acid. I said no, one thing led to another and we were to wander the streets of Portsmouth till dawn.

Lysergic Acid Diethylamide or LSD for short was created by a Swiss Chemist in 1938. He discovered its hallucinogenic properties by accident, on his way home on a bike, and remarked on how it enhanced his senses.

'Acid' became a favourite for what became known as the Beat Generation, and it became fashionable for the hippy movement of the 1950s and 60s to go on LSD-induced trips. In Portsmouth it was the summer of Green Acid, and the single drop on the sugar cube in Tony Nabarro's fridge meant that for a month I could not see a red bus or pillar box without reaching for my sunglasses. Many have tried, but I think it impossible to describe a typical trip, simply because there isn't one. Front-runners of the so-called Beat Generation like WS Burroughs and Jack Kerouac have written about drug-fuelled experiences; for me I would just say how much more clearly, I seemed to see things under the influence of acid. In particular I remember when, just as we passed my old home in Castle Road, my guide paused, bent over and picked something up from the gutter. He held the ice lolly stick up for a moment, then dropped it back into the gutter. Then he smiled knowingly and said: 'Saturday Morning Picture Club.' It was a literally magical moment and he and the acid had transported me back in time. Almost instantly, I was back there at the Essoldo, cheering on The Lone Ranger and screaming with laughter at Laurel and Hardy while throwing the peel from my orange at the arm-banded and torch-bearing children who acted as aisle monitors, or Little Hitlers as we called them.

I didn't actually think or believe I was there, I just remembered it so clearly and felt all the emotions of the five-year-old I thought I had outgrown and left behind.

For the next four hours we walked through empty streets and along the promenade in search of sea monsters and ghostly reminders of the city's past. It was certainly a trip to remember, and it has never left me.

A few years after my Pompey Trip I would share Tony's apartment in Kings Road when his lovely, talented and almost unbelievably tolerant wife Marilyn was dancing her way around Europe.

It was an interesting experience, as visitors like Cottage Grove Pete, Shane the Wanderer and Little or Big Dylan would softly tap the entry code out on the door at any time of night or day. Whatever the time, there would be much philosophising and conspicuous consumption while listening to suitable drug-taking anthems.

This was towards the end of my drug-indulgent days. I was still taking substances at gigs and would sometimes act as an unpaid messenger by picking up and delivering small amounts of cannabis resin to ladies at the Pomme and surrounding pubs. It was a good year for Lebanese Gold I remember, and I could carry four Oxo-cube-sized lumps at a time in my mouth. This was in case of apprehension by DS Dave 'Hoppy' Hopkins and his fellow members of the Portsmouth Drug Squad. Dave was always dapper in his Crombie overcoat, crisp white shirt and Perry Como haircut, and a genuinely nice bloke. He knew I was only playing at the game.

The trip with Tony was to be my last dabble with other mind-altering substances, except, of course, scrumpy cider.

~

A big Rolling Stones hit at this time was *(It's) All Over Now*. For my band, that was literally true. The Stormriders would storm no more, and I would have to find fame and fortune through some other medium.

The final straw was the fiasco of our big break on the stage of the Savoy. The irony was that the band had abstained from taking any drugs before the performance, and instead of playing better, we played much worse. I lost a couple of strings during the manic finale of *Whole Lotta Shaking*, and overuse of the echo chamber made it impossible to follow the tune for us as well as the audience. After the echoes and the boos subsided, the judges debated briefly and named the winning act.

Being beaten by a twelve-year-old boy trumpeter playing a selection of songs from South Pacific was too much to bear for us all. There was to be no official analysis or final meeting; we just went our ways and never played together again.

To finally underscore that my rock 'n' roll days were over, I lost my Grimshaw SS Deluxe guitar. For some unthinking reason, I lent it to little Ginger Barber, he of the cauliflower ear, cheeky grin and more tattoos than I ever saw on one human being. He said he was going away on a job and wanted to learn the guitar and entertain his workmates during the long evenings. In spite of the weakness of his story and still stunned by our loss of face at The Savoy, I simply handed it over and never saw it or him again. I found out later that Ginger had pawned it for a tenth of its value, and by then it was too late for me to redeem it.

It was a sad and symbolic end to the year, and I think it finally brought home to me that I had neither the application nor temperament, let alone the ability to become a rock god. I would have to find something else I could be good at.

1965

- ~ Cigarette advertising is banned from British television
- ~ Sir Winston Churchill dies at the age of 90
- ~ The Beatles second film *Help* is released
- ~ African-American human rights activist Malcolm X visits Smethwick after the racially charged 1964 election
- ~ Malcolm X is assassinated in New York
- ~ Golden eagle 'Goldie' is recaptured after twelve days of freedom from London Zoo
- ~ Cosmonaut Alexei Leonov makes the first walk in space
- ~ Scottish racing driver Jim Clark wins the Indianapolis 500 and the F1 World Driving Championship
- ~ Bob Dylan causes controversy by using an electric guitar at the Newport Folk Festival
- ~ Edward Heath becomes the leader of the Conservative Party
- ~ The Beatles perform at the world's first music stadium concert at New York, attracting a crowd of 55,000
- ~ The classic sci-fi serial *Thunderbirds* debuts on ITV

~ Stock Clerk, Ian Brady is charged with the killing of 17-year-old Edward Evans at the start of investigations into what will become known as The Moors Murders
~ The first album by The Who *(My Generation)* is released

Top Tunes

I Got You Babe ~ Sonny and Cher
(I Can't Get No) Satisfaction ~ The Rolling Stones
Like a Rolling Stone ~ Bob Dylan
I Fought the Law ~ Bobby Fuller Four
Woolly Bully ~ Sam the Sham and The Pharoes
In The Midnight Hour ~ Wilson Pickett
Papa's Got a Brand New Bag ~ James Brown
Mr Tambourine Man ~ The Byrds
These Boots are Made for Walkin' ~ Nancy Sinatra
(I'm a) Road Runner ~ Junior Walker and the All
Stars
Yesterday ~ The Beatles
The Sounds of Silence ~ Simon and Garfunkel
Ticket to Ride ~ The Beatles
California Dreamin' ~ The Mamas and Papas
Unchained Melody ~ The Righteous Brothers
Hang on Sloopy ~ The McCoys
Stop! in the Name of Love ~ The Supremes
Mrs. Brown You've Got a Lovely Daughter ~
Herman and the Hermits
Elusive Butterfly (of Love) ~ Bob Lind
Groovy Kind of Love ~ The Mindbenders
King of the Road ~ Roger Miller
It's Not Unusual ~ Tom Jones

Trailers for sale or rent
Rooms to let, 50 cents
No phone, no pool, no pets
I ain't got no cigarettes
Ah, but two hours of pushing broom
Buys a eight by twelve four-bit room
I'm a man of means, by no means
King of the road

King of the Road, written and performed by Roger Miller

~

We were in the midst of the so-called Swinging Sixties and times were certainly a-changing. But while the genie of liberalism was struggling to get out of the bottle, the Establishment still had a tight grip on the cork. We still hanged people, the Rolling Stones were fined for peeing against a petrol station wall, and PJ Proby would split his trousers on stage and be removed from public consciousness.

~

At last I had my freedom, but what to do with it?

After five years of having no choice but waste my days on building sites, my apprenticeship was over and I was free to do all the things I'd dreamed of while joining pipes together.

Then I saw the Catch 22 in my situation.

Quite simply, I had no money to do all the exciting things I was now free to do. If I wanted to explore exotic places beyond the Isle of Wight, I would need the money I would not be earning. And I was, as usual, boracic (lint-skint-broke). I had made no provision for rainy or sunny days, which was to be a recurring theme in my life.

As bigamists know, leading a double life does not come cheap. Nor does pretending to be rich, and I'd always lived to and beyond the limit of my means. Whereas brother John had Mother's business acumen and instincts, I followed my dad and had lived life to the full with no thought of putting something away for my future adventures. In short, I was potless.

It was all very well deciding to jump on a ferry and set up as a starving artist in a Parisian garret, but even starving artists had to pay the rent. If I wanted to travel to exotic foreign parts, I could follow John's example and use my qualifications to bluff my way into a job in the Merchant Navy. But now I was free to do so I didn't like the idea of taking orders, having no say on where I was going, and being stuck on a boat with a lot of people I might otherwise not have chosen to spend my days and nights with. I liked the idea of meeting a rich widow with a heart condition on a cruise liner, but not what it would take to become a gigolo.

The one thing I was sure of was that I wanted to take a look at other lands before settling on my next move towards worldwide fame and fortune. I fancied the idea of being a king of the road in a nice warm climate, but even hitchhiking my way from place to place would have to be paid for.

Then a mate came up with the solution.

For the past year, Bill had been my mate in work and play...and in battle.

Although no bigger than me, Bill was much stronger,

and had bailed me out on several occasions when I had taken on superior forces. On one occasion, I'd managed to provoke a whole posse of tractor boys at a concert in Salisbury Town Hall. Paul Jones and the Manfred Mann band had stopped performing and watched in almost admiration as Bill steamed in and dragged me from the ruck and out of the emergency exit. He was a good man to have at your back, and based on past performances was known to admirers as One-Punch Willy.

Because I'd left the company, Bill was also out of work. Then, after a week of idleness, he called to say he had found what sounded like a perfect opportunity for us to build up a pot. Ironically, it meant juggling with pipes for a few months longer, but it was a big payer and we would both be in funds.

Bill's sister lived in London, and had spotted and sent him an advertisement for pipe fitter and mate pairs for a three-month contract. As well as a London-weighted hourly rate, there would also be allowances for accommodation, travelling and out-of-pocket expenses. The interesting bit was that the job was putting in the heating for a college being built just outside Portsmouth. As he said, all we had to do was pretend to be living at his sister's house in Clapham, and be agreeable to work away in Hampshire if the price was right. Was I on? I was, and within a week we had been for an interview and got the job.

After ceremonially burning my overalls, getting to grips with pipes again was not exactly what I'd planned, but it was a way to build up funds for my adventures in foreign parts.

~

With a generous accommodation allowance during the contract, it seemed a good idea for me to try living away from home for the first time. I loved living with my parents and being looked after by Mother, but I felt I needed to prove to myself that I could be self-sufficient.

There were no tears, but Mother was clearly upset that her youngest son was leaving, even if my new residence was only round the corner.

I suppose she was even more unhappy as my brother had technically moved out the month before. Making big money at a time when so many people were buying cars for the first time, John had bought himself what we then called a bachelor pad. His new home was a small but swish cottage in Garden Lane, just yards away from the back entrance to the house in St Edwards Road. As he said, it was not really like leaving home as he would be over for meals as usual. As I said to Mother, I would be a more than frequent guest and would always be happy to join the family for a meal and to drop my dirty washing in. She said that she understood I had reached an age when I wanted my own place and to look after myself, and that there was a new laundromat in Castle Road.

The evening before my departure, John joined us in the small sitting room on the first floor. I occasionally dream they are still there, with Mother knitting in between ferrying food and drinks from the kitchen. *Hancock's Half Hour* is on the television, and dad is making a Digger Shag roll-up, with the pouch on his lap and his impossibly long legs stretched out and his feet resting possessively on Sputnick, the Jack Russell Terrier. Named for the Russian satellite which hit the headlines with its launch in 1957, Sput is getting on now, and it will break my father's heart when she goes. Sitting in a halo of bay rum and expensive aftershave, brother John is wearing his toff-at-rest cardigan, cravat and cavalry twill trousers ensemble and looking through the *Portsmouth News* to see what his fellow car dealers are offering.

The strange thing is, when I wake from a dream, I seem to smell the mixture of strong tobacco and bay rum. I can hear the slow tick of the old Napoleon clock on the mantelpiece, Sputnick's snores and the comforting click of Mother's knitting needles. Silly, but I believe that all the time I dream of them they will still be there in that room and in my heart

~

The Gaye Flatlets were situated in a former hotel on a road overlooking Southsea Common. Occupying the basement was The Gaye Toros bar, dressed throughout with red lights, red cloaks and fake bulls' heads and posters for *corridas* that would never happen. I don't know where the surplus 'e' in 'Gaye' came from, but perhaps the owners thought it gave the place an exotic ring. For sure, whoever did the signage above the doors was not going to put the new proprietors straight on their spelling ability, as they were heavyweight London gangsters.

East London had the Kray Twins; the Regan brothers' manor was south of the river.

Rumour had it that the brothers bought the building

as an investment with some of their ill-gotten gains, and I apologise profusely to them if the story is untrue.

To be honest, there was a certain cache to be paying rent to South London gangsters, and we were to have an interesting time at the Gaye Flatlets. We were also earning so much that we were able to live in some style and still put money away. I would give my savings to Mother each week to ensure they were beyond my reach.

By day we would be at work on what was to become Havant Sixth Form College; each evening, we would scrub up and put on our finery and prepare for a night on the tiles with drinks and a meal in the Gaye Toros. The manageress was the lovely Hazel Pople, married to a mate and with a heart of pure gold unless someone took liberties. Our standard meal was steak and chips, garnished with a fried egg, peas and Hazel's incomparable onion rings. That set us back eight shillings apiece (forty pence) and set us up for a night of roistering in Southsea's square mile. In case of exposure as a pipe fitter rather than a brain surgeon, member of the Cadbury family or whatever the latest tale was, The Pomme D'Or Club was off limits. If we did bump into a member of the Southsea jet set, I would introduce Bill as a pilot with TWA. He had worked on enough planes for the airline to know all about what went where on the flight deck, and could be quite convincing unless he had a gin and tonic too many and started telling tales of touching down with one engine on fire or disarming an intruder into the cockpit with a spare hand.

~

Because of who owned the bar, misbehaviour at the Gaye Toros was unusual. I remember one group of local would-be gangsters offering to look after the place until they were told who they were trying to get protection money from.

Another time, I was having a drink with a couple of acquaintances when a stag night arrived and took exception to my face. There were seven of them and only three of us, but I reckoned each of my companions was worth at least two of them. They were, and the battle was short if bloody. The walking wounded dragged their comatose mates up the stairs, and the regulars put the tables and chairs back in place.

One of my fighting friends was a fellow resident, and a former inmate of HM Prison Parkhurst where he spent several years as a result of robbing a casino. Jack was a renowned scrapper, and his appearance made more intimidating by a scar across his cheek and an ill-fitting glass eye. He was known as One-Eyed Jack, but nobody used the nickname in his presence unless they were sure how it would be taken.

My other comrade-at-arms was the Demon Barber of Southsea. Unlike Jack, Des was quite happy with his sobriquet, as he had a dark sense of humour. He once showed me a souvenir of his time in the Royal Marines. The grainy photograph showed a group of bare-chested soldiers in baggy khaki shorts. They were grinning at the camera as a younger Des held a lighter flame to a cigarette stuck in the mouth of a human head. He explained that the photo had been taken when the British Government employed Dayak natives to find and kill members of the Malayan Liberation Army.

After leaving the Marines, Des had set up as a hairdresser in Southsea. He was surprisingly gentle and considerate while wielding scissors and comb, but still carried a cut-throat razor in his waistcoat pocket while out... and had been known to use it. He pulled his coat back to show it once when we were in the toilet of the Gaye Toros. As we stood side-by-side at the urinal, he said in his soft voice that there was a rumour going round that I had grassed up a mutual mate who had robbed a Post Office van in Old Portsmouth. I was much relieved when he said he of course did not believe it, and would think about cutting the rumour spreader's tongue out.

~

In between looking after the family's business interests elsewhere, Danny Regan was a frequent visitor to Portsmouth, and we would meet occasionally in the Gaye Toros bar.

I remember how he would walk carefully down the steps to the bar with steady, precise steps and looking more like an accountant that a gangster with his dark suit and tie, neat haircut and Michael Caine-style spectacles. He would always be accompanied by his minder, who seemed to be at least as wide as he was tall. He wore a deep scar down one side of his face, and was said to have been involved in a shooting at a night club in London during a disturbance involving the Kray and Richardson gangs, and which left a man dead.

When Danny arrived on the premises, he would

always invite me to have a drink, and I was always quick to accept and be humbly grateful.

~

Our stay at the Gaye Flatlets ended with the signing-off of the job at Havant, and coincided with my arriving at my bedsit to find a very large man sitting on my bed. He was wearing a long overcoat and a pleasant smile, and I couldn't help but notice he was holding a small revolver in his left hand. It was probably not that small, but his giant hand made it look as if it were.

As his warrant card confirmed, my visitor was a senior Inspector in the city's Criminal Investigation Department, and he said he'd found the gun in the pocket of my jacket in the wardrobe.

I said I had never seen it before, and he smiled even more pleasantly and said I would say that, wouldn't I?

He went on to say he and his colleagues were investigating a number of armed robberies in and around the city, and the gun matched the description given by a bank employee who had had it pointed at her.

I said that I should imagine one revolver looked much like another, and if his fingerprints had not got in the way, I was sure they would find that mine were not on it.

To this he shrugged as if not bothered about such details, and said if the gun was not mine I must know who it belonged to. Unless I gave him the owner's name and those of his accomplices, I could be going down for a very long stretch. Armed robbery was not common in Portsmouth and, he added as an extra dig, far more serious than beating a local bobby up.

Trying to sound more confident and unconcerned than I felt, I said I had been too busy welding pipes together to be involved in any armed robberies in recent times, and knew nobody who was.

Our conversation continued for a while, then he heaved himself up off the bed, and left, assuring me that I would hear from him or a colleague soon. As he left, I asked if he was not going to give me the gun back, but he didn't seem to get the joke.

I learned later that my friend and fellow resident Bill had been taken to Southsea police station and been given a similar grilling before being released. We heard later that a couple of fellow residents at the Gaye Flatlets had been found guilty of the robberies and sent down for a long stretch. Luckily, we also heard that they knew that it was neither Bill nor I who had put them in the frame.

~

I was now tooled-up with enough money to see me through several months wherever I chose to roam in foreign parts, and decided it was a good time to embark on my own Grand Tour. This was a tradition established in the 18th Century, when young gentlemen of sufficient means and suitable class would mark their 21st birthdays by taking luxurious transport around the capitals of Europe, typically accompanied by a tutor. I came within the 21st birthday category, but would be travelling on my thumb, and my companion would be one of the regulars at The Bridge Tavern.

Johnny Parkinson was an immensely likeable and easy-going young man who liked the idea of hitching our way through a few European hot-spots during the summer months. He had just left one job and had saved enough not to be in a hurry to find another.

Over a few pints in the Bridge, we decided to keep it simple and cheap. We would buy some camping gear and suitable clothing from the ex-WD stores in Fratton Road, board a ferry and then decide where to go when we arrived in France.

Listening in to our plans, Harry the landlord said in case we decided not to come back or got killed we should mark our departure with a leaving party, which could double up with my 21st birthday celebration. I pointed out that I had already had a 21st birthday celebration, of which I had no recollection until waking up in my bed with a re-broken nose and a bloody shirtfront, cradling a sink complete with taps which appeared to have come from a public toilets.

To this, Harry riposted that as I had no memory of the previous one, a repeat would be in order, and we should make it a special occasion.

Thus was the Great Mystery Tour Disaster conceived.

~

Tickets were soon on sale at the Bridge for the mystery coach trip, but even with the chicken-in-a-basket meal and entertainment promised, the take-up was modest. It was, I think, me who decided the offer should be extended to non-regulars, and to make the very bad decision to sell tickets to pubs where other groups of tough young men liked to gather.

Over the next week, I visited pubs in and around the city and sold the remaining tickets with no problem. What I didn't take into account was the almost inevitable outcome of putting sixty tearaways from a handful of dodgy pubs all together for a booze cruise.

~

It was to be the first time I appeared in court as a witness for the prosecution rather than a defendant.

The destination for our mystery tour was a quiet country pub near Southampton, and we arrived mid-evening after six stops for refreshments on route. This was during a journey of less than twenty miles, and though pleased with the addition to the evening's takings, the landlords were also obviously glad to see the coach trundle out of the car park.

The trouble started when the chicken and chips in a basket was late in arriving, and the stripper I'd booked failed to show. As if to signal the start of the fracas, an explosion rocked the toilets; it was the result of detonating a small improvised explosive device which one of our number had chosen to make and bring along in case it came in handy. It all kicked off when one of the boys from The Greyhound at Leigh Park asked if the girlfriend of a local would like to dance. The fact he was not wearing any trousers upset the local, and the fracas started.

When I was summoned by the prosecution as a

material witness, the local police sergeant told me that it was a big event for them, as they normally had more cases of pig rustling than mass brawls.

After the day in court and the sentencing of those charged with affray (the identity of the toilet bomber was never discovered) the police sergeant told me that there was talk of going after me as the organiser of what was bound to end in tears.

I had a pint with Johnny Parkinson, and we agreed it would be a good idea to start our tour of Europe sooner rather than later.

The view from the back seat of the car was of a stunningly beautiful landscape, but the ride through it was the closest I had as yet come to certain death.

High summer in the Central Massif area of France, and I and Johnny Parkinson, and our rucksacks were squeezed together in the back of a small and very dented Citroën Deux-Chevaux.

In the passenger seat, a pleasant-faced middle-aged-lady was calmly knitting and practising her English on us. In the driving seat was an elderly lady with one leg. Protruding from her flowery summer dress, the false one appeared to be no more than a shiny steel tube ending in a rubber stopper.

Rather than driving more cautiously because of her handicap, she was keeping up a furious pace down a corkscrew of winding and very narrow roads. Worse, there was only a low barrier between us and eternity. We were in prime wine-making territory, and the slopes of the mountains were lined with row after row of grape vines. It was a breath-taking panorama, but most of our breaths were taken in the form of gasps every time we hurtled round a blind corner.

As a giant lorry blared a warning and Madame nonchalantly steered us to the very edge of the abyss and to keep my mind from our situation, I asked the lady how her mother had lost her leg.

'Oh, you know,' she said as the needles clacked busily, 'just like this...when she was driving...'

~

Signature of bearer
Signature du titulaire.............. *P W Coot* ....

Signature of wife

*Photograph of
wife*

FOREIGN EXCHANGE FOR TRAVELLING EXPENSES

PREVIOUSLY ISSUED

Date	Amount	

NEW ISSUES OR REFUNDS

Date	*Amount issued or refunded* (sterling equivalent to nearest £1)	*Stamp of bank or travel agent*
12.5.65	£50	THOS. COOK & SON, LTD 9, PALMERSTON ROAD, SOUTHSEA, PORTSMOUTH

I suspect most people going on a walking tour of Europe would have made some degree of preparation and a rough itinerary. Many would have equipped themselves with maps and guides and phrase books. We had set off for the ferry from Southampton with our rucksacks and camping gear, our passports and a mix of cash and travellers' cheques. I also had a copy of *Europe on Five Dollars a Day*, a popular guide on where to find the cheapest food and accommodation. I'd picked it up in a second-hand bookshop and it was five years out of date, but I figured prices would not have changed that much. To see us through the trip we each had £50 in travellers cheques and twenty pounds' worth of French francs. When that ran out, we planned to look for casual work or go home. As John said, if times got really hard we could always sell our bodies in Paris, or rob a bank. As he also said, not knowing what lay ahead or how far we would get before circumstance forced our return or to take desperate measures was part of the fun.

Our plan was to head south for the French Riviera, and once there decide on turning right for Spain or left for Italy. I hadn't told John, but once on the Mediterranean coast, I planned to go in search of my long-time fantasy lover, the Sex Kitten. Brigitte Bardot was said to spend her summers on the Riviera, and after years of worshipping her on screen, I wanted to see her in the flesh. If I did, I would ask for an autograph and get John to take some photos of us so I could tell lies in the pub about making mad love to her on a sandy beach under a sky full of stars. At least, that was the plan.

After landfall at Le Havre and knowing the capital

was roughly to the south, we had followed the signs for Paris. Then, as we were to find was a common trick played on motorists, the signs petered out. We must then have wandered off-route and found ourselves on a little-used country road which eventually became no more than a lane.

Using the sun as a rough guide, we walked on through hamlets and villages, and people would come out of their homes to watch us go by. Things were different in those days, and two young foreigners with cropped blond hair, military outfits and carrying large rucksacks was obviously a curiosity. Or, as John said, sparked memories of the Occupation.

We held our thumbs up for every vehicle, but the tractors and lorries and one old bus full of school-children were only local traffic. Eventually and as dusk fell, we set up camp on the verge, dining on sandwiches and Wagon Wheels before climbing into our sleeping bags. We hadn't made much progress, but at least our adventure had begun. Laying on my back and looking up at the huge Norman sky, I reflected that, on the whole, I would rather be here on the road than on a Hampshire building site, the Gaye Flatlets or, especially, in Winchester remand centre.

~

We were woken just after dawn by a representative of the country's police force. He was a tall, smartly dressed motorcyclist who, having heard our plans, explained that we were actually further away from the Mediterranean than when we'd started. This road led to nowhere much but, eventually, Brittany. Our best chance of a lift to the Riviera would be on the main route south.

He gave us directions, wished us good luck and roared off, probably wondering how, if we were a fair example of the flower of English youth, our country had ever won the war.

~

The friendly *gendarme* was right, and we got a lift within an hour of arriving at the then main autoroute south.

For the next three days we walked and hitched, or caught buses and trains when it rained, covering around a hundred miles a day and sleeping where we could pitch the tents. It was totally different from anything either of us had experienced, and not at all like Pompey and the surrounding countryside.

In the heartland of this great country, we stood in mountaintop villages and looked across a landscape of dead volcanoes, gorges and lush valleys. We rode on narrow-gauge, single-track railways, looking out on regimented lines of grapevines and fields ablaze with sunflowers. While the landscape has remained unchanged, rural life in France was decidedly different six decades ago. Farming machinery was uncommon, and I remember seeing a man in a striped jersey and beret, holding on to a wooden plough and shouting encouragement to the giant ox pulling it.

On through the endless and eternal landscape, and our journey took us through tiny villages and past fortresses and fairy-tale castles as we sampled the local dishes, cheeses and, of course, wine.

It left memories I will always recall fondly, even the morning when the little red and white car screeched to a stop and the lady with the knitting needles asked if we would like a lift. They were going all the way to the sea, she said, and we were welcome to accompany them. It would help with her English, and our conversation would help keep Mama awake at the wheel.

~

According to my out-of-date guide book, nude bathing on the Isle of Levant was not so much allowed as actively encouraged.

Having done my homework, I knew that La Brigitte was known to be a visitor. It was too much to hope she would be there and free of a swimming costume when we arrived, but I figured it was worth a shot.

Hyeres was and is a resort town on the French Riviera, and the beach looked like it had been designed and created specifically to be photo-graphed for tourist posters. We arrived hot and dusty and still shaking from our ride with the Mad Madame, and thought we were in Heaven. Used to the pebbly windswept beach at Southsea, we found ourselves ankle-deep in warm, golden sand which was dotted with palm trees, parasols, open-air bars and beautiful, tanned young women slinking around, sunbathing or posing artfully with beach balls aloft.

Some, unlike what one would expect to see on the beach at Southsea, were topless.

Not even bothering to ask the price, we pitched our pup tents next to a likely looking bar. A real bonus was that we were to be adopted by the owner of the beachside campsite. Pierre was a wealthy, middle-aged Corsican with a great tan and a pigtail, who spent his days in shorts and flip flops, expensive shades and a stylish straw hat. He was, as is not always the case with French people, a great Anglophile, and chauffeured us around the sights, hot spots and places to be seen in his snow-white Jaguar E-type convertible.

The only disappointment was that the sex kitten was not currently to be found on the Isle of Levant. As our host said, if Bardot was not there, why bother to cross the water to see a few naked girls when there were so many to hand on the mainland?

We agreed and stayed on for a wonderful week of sun, sea, sand and, on an almost daily basis, sex.

~

Though reluctant to leave this demi-paradise, we decided that if we wanted to see more of Europe before our money ran out, it was time to move on.

John was all for heading westward to the Costa del Sol, but we tossed a coin and, as I cheated, I got my way. Our route to the glories of Rome and the snow-clad slopes of Switzerland would take us along the Riviera hot spots, and, more particularly, The Sex Kitten's home turf of St Tropez.

~

It was in one of the ritziest towns along the Riviera that we discovered the delights of the Youth Hostel Association and what we had been missing on the way south.

The YHA was set up in the early years of the 20th century to provide cheap accommodation for young, working people on walking breaks. By the Sixties, there were hostels around the world. They were clean, comfortable and cheap at the equivalent of twenty pence a night. Even better, some had dormitories shared by both sexes. They were also often in prime locations.

In Nice, the hostel was close to the beach and the prom, but unfortunately not gender neutral. In those days and compared with liberal French attitudes, there was strict supervision and even a curfew with doors locked at ten pm sharp. Fortunately for us there was scaffolding all around the building, so we were able to get back in to not only our dormitory, but the one reserved for female occupation.

~

Known as The Pearl of France, Menton is the last resort before the border with Italy. It was also my last chance to catch up with Brigitte Bardot, who was rumoured to be filming in the area with Anthony Perkins. Our rendezvous was not to be, but we did meet the Korean actor who played Oddjob, the villain's minder in the *Goldfinger* Bond movie. My small claim to celeb fame is that he not only gave me his autograph on a paper napkin, but accepted my challenge to an arm-wrestle. He smiled and continued to munch away casually at his ham baguette while I struggled with both hands to move his free one. It would have been a photo opportunity to match my planned liaison with Brigitte Bardot, but John forgot to take the cap off his Box Brownie.

For the next fortnight, we walked and hitched our way through Italy, having small adventures in big cities. In Milan, we coincided with the derby between the city's two soccer teams, but failed to talk our way in as sports reporters from a mythical English fanzine.

In Venice we wandered across St Mark's Square, took water buses along the Grand Canal and swam in the Lido. I've not been back since, but my memory is of a city of great contrasts. In particular when we stood and gagged on the sweet smell of sewage as turds and condoms bobbed along the canal past the magnificent Doge's Palace and towards the Bridge of Sighs.

In Pisa we ate futtanta garlic bread and took turns to pose for the usual tourist photos of each of us apparently holding onto and preventing the Leaning Tower from leaning any further.

In Florence we stayed in a once-magnificent palazzo on the banks of the Arno River and earned some much-needed lire by flogging badly-cured leather bags at the Ponte Vecchio on commission from a local market trader. He spoke no more English than we did Italian, but obviously thought two young British men would be better than him at selling souvenirs to elderly women tourists. In this he was right. It was my first experience of being bought dinner and plied with drinks by a woman older than my mother, but in our situation, we needed all the financial help we could get.

Zig-zagging across country to Rimini, we found and booked into a YHA hostel overlooking the golden sands of this popular resort. As elsewhere, the hostel was in as enviable a location as the five-star hotel alongside, and a fraction of the cost. As in southern France, we spent our days lounging around on the beach and working on our tans and the girls. The problem was our total ignorance of Italian, except for *ciao,* pizza, spaghetti, *grazie, si, no* and *sei cosi sexy* ('you are so sexy').

When we did find someone who knew what we were talking about, our line was that we were a couple of film company executives on the lookout for locations and likely background artists for the next 007 movie. We were staying at the five-star hotel on the prom, and if they were interested in being a Bond girl we could meet them in the bar that evening. If it happened and we got on well, we could not of course invite them back to the hostel next door, so would suggest a moonlight walk and perhaps some role play for the steamier bits of the forthcoming blockbuster movie.

~

Rome, and we stood in the Colosseum and tried to imagine the roar of the crowd as the lions were let loose on the Christians and clubbed together to buy a single ice cream by the Trevi Fountain.

Then minor tragedy struck.

Lying on my bed in the hostel, I was consulting my *Europe on Five Dollars a Day* to find the cheapest place for a bowl of spaghetti when I heard an agonised bellow. John was in the shower and I guessed he had set the temperature of the water at too hot. When I went to investigate, I found it to be not unlike the shower scene in *Psycho*, but with my mate playing the Janet Leigh role. Blood was running in streams down the tiled walls and swirling into the plug hole, and John was hanging on to the shower curtain with eyes shut and face distorted in pain. When I'd sluiced him down and helped him out of the shower, he explained the problem. Whether because of all those nights sleeping on damp grass, the long miles of walking in between lifts, or even the unaccustomed diet of no meat and not much else but pasta, his farmer Giles's had exploded.

I felt his pain in both senses of the term and offered to help push the bleeding piles back to where they belonged. My offer was refused and a doctor called in. He said the technical term for what had happened was thrombosed haemorrhoids, supplied some ointment and earnestly recommended John abandon the tour and return home to recover.

It was a painful blow for him in more ways than one. I offered to escort him back to Pompey, but he insisted I go on alone. When I saw him off at the station, he gave me his spare cash. I said I would pay him back as soon as I could, but he said not to worry. All he wanted from me was a promise I would not tell the boys at The Bridge why he had decided to come home early. Better that they think we had fallen out than know about the *Psycho* scene and his exploding piles.

~

I woke to a pervasive odour that smelled as if a hundred cats had been peeing in the same room. It was dark, and apart from knowing I was in Geneva, I had absolutely no idea of exactly where I was or how I had got there. Beneath me I could feel a bed of loose straw, and my head felt as if it was in danger of falling off. Then, I heard a low, rumbling growl and saw a large pair of green eyes regarding me through the gloom.

I shook my head and looked again, and saw that the owner of the eyes was a very large lion, and that he did not seem pleased to see me. Luckily, we were on opposite sides of the bars of the cage, and my best move seemed to be to crawl quietly away and under the flap of the tent in which I had obviously spent the night.

Later and recuperating in the bar with a bottle of the same very rough red that had done the damage, Griselda stroked my forehead and explained who she was and how I had come to spend the night with Umberto and his harem.

The Zoppa family circus was moving on, and I had spent the day working with the other casual labour roustabouts, taking down and packing away the big top. I'd literally stumbled across Griselda while she was going through her warm-up exercises outside her caravan. After watching in awe as she put her head between her legs and hopped across the grass on her hands, I asked her bottom if she fancied a drink. One bottle had led to another and we had eventually retired to her caravan. After an hour of her showing me some extremely unusual and inventive positions, she said I said I was going to join the circus and spend the rest of my life with her, then set off in search of the ringmaster to enlist as a lion tamer. She had eventually found me in the big cat tent and, not being able to wake me, made me comfortable and left.

After a near-tearful farewell, I stood and waved to Griselda as the circus moved on. I sometimes think of her and wonder how and where she is, and if she can still wrap those long and lissom limbs completely around her swan-like neck.

~

Apart from long spells between lifts or the risk of being sexually assaulted or murdered by your host, the thing about hitchhiking is that you need to be adaptable as to your destination and route. The upside is that you get to know so many interesting people you would otherwise never have got to meet.

John and I had made a very wobbly snail trail around Italy, and after his departure I'd found myself in Switzerland's second-most populous city. My host had been an American born-again Christian pastor on his way to a conference for believers from around the world. On the journey he made several attempts to get me to change my religious views and sexual orientation, was unsuccessful at both, but gave me his contact details in case I changed my mind.

After a week of washing up in scrupulously clean or filthy restaurant kitchens and stealing leftover food from plates and even bins when nobody was looking, I decided it was time to move on. I had my last swim beneath the giant fountain, packed my haversack and held my thumb up on the busy ring road.

My next host was a villainous looking but friendly English long-distance driver. Curiously, he'd been delivering allegedly Italian designer shoes to Rome from London, and nodded to where several boxes sat on the dashboard. They were, he said, an aide to progress if he were stopped by the Polizia Stradale motorway cops. It gave him some pleasure that he was bribing them with knock-off big name shoes which had been churned out in a sweat shop in Stepney. A lot of British people thought badly of their police force, he said, but they had nothing on Italian cops for bribery and corruption.

After a long and companionable journey. Dusty handed me a handful of Lire and dropped me off at a motorway stop. I didn't have long to wait by the pumps before I was almost immediately picked up by a jolly middle-class family on route to a friend's holiday home in a mountain village in Austria.

It was strange to find myself in my lightweight gear in the then little-known skiing resort of Lech. Unsurprisingly there was no YHA hostel, and I was thinking of headlines in the local news about a frozen body found in a tent, when I saw a B & B advertisement on the wall of a bar. At ten bob even off-season, it was twice the price of a night in a hostel, but better than sleeping *al fresco*. The kindly lady owner of the picture-postcard chalet gave me tea and cakes and offered me access to the shower and her absent son's pyjamas. She was amused by my tales of travel, and even more so when I said goodnight, then came back down the stair and said I thought she had forgotten to put any sheets or a counterpane on the bed.

It was my first encounter with a duvet, known then in Britain as a Continental Quilt and familiar only to well-travelled and trendy folk in the Home Counties.

I had dreamed long ago of picturesque starvation in a Parisian garret, and now found myself starving in a tent in the Bois de Boulogne. It was not as much fun as I'd imagined.

I had left Austria and arrived in Paris with a little over five shillings in francs in my pocket. The travellers' cheques and John's parting gift had gone, and I really was on my uppers after walking and riding a distance of around 3000 miles in a couple of months. The summer season was on the wing, and I spent the next three days unsuccessfully trudging around Montmartre and trying to find casual work in the bars and restaurants. I even tried sitting next to someone else's pavement art with my cap beside me, but was chased off when the real author returned from lunch.

I stuck it for three days, living off stale baguettes and croissants which the French considered inedible after a couple of hours after they had emerged from the oven.

They would not sell them at reduced rates, so I would steal them from the bins behind the bakeries, probably doing a few pigs out of their rights. In stories with happy endings, a rich heiress or patron will turn up at the last moment, but it didn't work that way.

Deeply ashamed, I phoned Mother and told her the situation.

Within a few hours she had sent money by the *poste restante* system for the train and boat fares, and, of course, for food.

For a long moment I thought to head for Les Deux

*Magots** for a blow-out, then saw sense, walked away from the tent and headed for the next boat train.

~

Les Deux Magots was a bar and restaurant of choice for the capital's intellectual and artistic community. The likes of Jean-Paul Sartre, Ernest Hemmingway, Pablo Picasso, Albert Camus and James Joyce all liked to pose there. Even in my day, it would have cost the entire rail and boat fare to have had a substantial meal there.
By the way, the name has nothing to do with maggots, but in context refers to two Chinese figurines on show.

~

Back in Pompey, I had a lot to think about.

I was living back home and in debt to Mother, and would need to sort myself out and get back on the road to fame and fortune. But for the moment, I also needed to record the experiences of the past two months and think about what I had learned from them.

I had certainly learned that hitchhiking could be fun or fearsome, and that sleeping rough, washing dishes and begging in European capitals was not as much fun as when you read about someone else doing it.

But, for sure, I had enjoyed some magic moments, met some interesting people and realised I loved being abroad. Just being where people spoke a different language and did things differently meant that everyday activities became a small adventure. Especially when trying to make way with a girl who you literally couldn't chat up.

Apart from all the times I was wet, cold, hungry and in fear of my safety, I had really enjoyed being footloose and fancy free. All I had to do now was find a way of affording being able to spend a lot more time on the other side of the English Channel.

~

After a lot of thought, I worked out that what I needed was a skill I could use anywhere and could live where I wanted. I'd tried being a rock god and *avante garde* painter and boxer and proved to myself I was rubbish at those activities. I certainly didn't want to go back on the tools and weld pipes together at home or abroad. Then it occurred to me that, apart from writing pornographic short stories at school and selling them to my class mates, I had never tried creative writing except for my brief spell at night school. I was an avid reader, so how hard could it be to make up stories?

I had kept a detailed diary of my adventures on the road in Europe, and would start by turning them, into a racy novel. If I got it right, it would be an instant best seller and I would be rich and famous, the two things I had been trying to achieve for the best part of a decade.

In the meantime, though, I would need to get a job.

Top of the Pops: 'King George' in action at the Sound Barrier.

Like other nightclubs in the city, the Sound Barrier had re-invented itself across the years

Opposite the footbridge across the main railway line and next door to the premises of a coal merchant, the club had begun life as Ricky's, named for the eldest son of the owners. There was a brief incarnation as the Romantica, with a plan to serve sophisticated meals and entertainment, but that was not to the public taste. Nowadays it was The Sound Barrier, and in the hands of Ricky's younger brother. With the predictable stage name of King George, I was the resident DJ. I was also an occasional barman and bouncer, and sometimes all three on the same night.

That took care of my evenings, but I needed a day job if I was to get a pot together to see me through the writing of my ground-breaking novel.

Soon and after a heavy night of putting discs on the turntable and throwing troublemakers out of the door, I would be up early to throw barrels of beer and high-octane scrumpy cider into the cellars of hundreds of Portsmouth pubs.

Despite the attentions of the *Luftwaffe* and city redevelopers, there was still the best part of a thousand pubs in Portsmouth. They varied from the posh ones like the Portland, to corner locals and even four-ale bars. The name of these old spit-and-sawdust boozers came not from the number of different draught beers they served, but the price of a pint in the previous century, which was four pence. Most ale or beer houses did not hold a licence to serve spirits, a measure brought in to try and cut back on the number of citizens who became addicted to cheap gin in the early Victorian era. Even in modern times there were still a couple of beer-only houses in Portsmouth, the Spread Eagle in Arundel Street being a memorable example.

I worked for the Brickwood Brewery company, and each morning I and my mate would load up dozens of five-gallon wooden tubs of rough cider. With a second load, we would make twenty or more "drops' a day, and be offered a pint in most of them. I knew drivers who could take eighteen pints of Brickwood Best and still drive fairly steadily back to the depot. My particular run included the Commercial Road pubs where I had been a regular customer in my Mr Hyde days. The thirst for scrumpy was prodigious. When the fleet was in, I would drop fifty tubs of scrumpy off at The Albany on a Friday, then take another twenty on Monday to see them through the week. That was coming up 3000 pints of gut-rot scrumpy a week, and from just that one pub. Billy Connolly used to remark on how pools of vomit on the pavements of Glasgow would always contain small chunks of carrot. In Pompey in those days, it was small chunks of cider apple.

~

I lasted as a club DJ for six months and a brewer's drayman for a year, then went mad. My problem was that as soon as I could do something, I got bored and quit.

Over the coming year I would try my hand at being a baker's roundsman, factory worker and grave-digger. I was a Corona lemonade man, and watched my flatbed lorry disappear under a swarm of kids when I delivered to Leigh Park. I even set up shop as a private detective and had just one case before having to retire from the business. This came about after I trailed a suspected unfaithful wife and watched from the vantage point of the garden shed as she had a wild sex session in the kitchen with a man in a black mask and wellington boots. It was only after showing the evidence to her husband that I learned that the mystery man she had been having sex with was him.

But my short-lived career as a gumshoe was to have a very happy ending.

I was renting a suitably dingy basement office in the city centre, and managed to play on the sympathy of a secretary in the posh solicitor's offices upstairs. She would sneak down the internal stairs, bringing coffee and tea, office supplies and even furniture. Then one day she asked if I would like to join her for lunch with her best friend. I said yes, and have since often thought how apparently unimportant decisions can have momentous outcomes.

Delilah took me to the Manhattan Coffee Bar in Palmerston Road and, quite truly, my knees went weak as I saw the vision awaiting our arrival. I knew she had to be mine for ever, and, poor girl, she was.

But again, dear reader, that's another story.

The King of Rock 'n' Roll

With no warning, we lost Elvis on August the 16th, 1977. He was just 42.

As with the assassination of President Kennedy, millions still remember exactly where they were when the King left us. I was at the local radio station, Radio Victory, and went straight into the recording studio to scrap the planned edition of my programme *Pompey Rock* and replace it with an hour devoted to Elvis hits. On the day, I remember looking from the studio window and watching a small crowd gather in the car park to listen to the show and share their sadness.

As well as remembering the announcement of his passing, I, and I bet many millions of fans can remember where I was and what I felt when I first heard the King sing. And what it did to my head and heart and body. At just short of six feet and with an inimitable voice and almost impossibly handsome, he was the perfect rock idol. Unlike poor Cliff, he could also move like no other. He really was sex on legs, and unbelievably, a really nice bloke. We boys didn't resent his captivation of all those millions of female fans. We just wanted to be him... or as much like him as we could manage. Most of us couldn't manage the looks, the voice or the leg movements, so we had to try to match the hair. My first Elvis quiff appeared when I was 13, and I was to spend the next five years trying to perfect it.

With sales of a billion records and more than thirty movies to his credit (some quite watchable), Elvis Aaron Presley was an ever-present influence in and on the lives of my generation. We lived and loved with and to his music, and for us, he truly was The King of Rock 'n' Roll.

Postscript

My sincere thanks for joining me on this journey through a time long gone. If you were around at this eruption of social and economic change, I hope my recollections have brought back a few pleasant memories.

For me it's been a quite often cathartic experience to recall, relate and thus re-live all those mistakes, thoughtless deeds, misadventures and potentially terminal wrong moves.

Like everyone else who gets to old age, I sometimes dwell on all the things I could and perhaps should have done differently. But then, as I say elsewhere, some small action or different direction taken could have led to tragedy, especially like not meeting my soul mate and ending up with such a wonderful family, the creation of which I played such a small part.

Thinking about it, I guess it's a mild disappointment that I never came close to making it as a rock god, internationally acclaimed artist or actor, but there are compensations a-plenty.

I remember how content my dear old dad was with his life with his soul mate and his journey from the Glasgow slums to his adopted city of Portsmouth. As he used to say, as long as you get through life without causing too much pain or damage to others, you've done alright. He also said that what he would like along with the details on his gravestone would be: *Just a Pompey Boy*. I reckon that will be good enough for me, too.

Minding your Language

(This item appeared in the first two episodes of my memoirs, but I figured it worth reproducing again for any new reader who might want a further insight into how we spoke and thought in those far-off days.)

Portsmouth is a treasure trove for anyone wanting to sample a whole range of dialects, slang and other alternative uses and abuses of the Queen's English. We Pomponians talk so funny for a number of reasons. To start with, the city has been a premier Naval port for many centuries and the Royal Navy has a language of its own. Also, generations of naval ratings arriving in Portsmouth from all parts of the British Isles have left their regional linguistic mark. Then there is the picaresque linkage with London, and Portsmouth has long been a popular stop-off point for travelling folk. All these elements have combined to create an often impenetrable argot (even to some locals) which blends rhyming slang, Romany, naval patois and all manner of regional dialects. Here's a sample of Pompey street-talk, which is bound to attract some controversy and disagreement. This is because words used and precise definition and even pronunciation can vary in different parts of the city. In fact, I have known Pompey families who have their own private language.

NB: *Please note the usual disclaimer that I am only the messenger of how we spoke in the Sixties, and did not invent or necessarily use the more offensive ways of describing people or places. It was another time, and as they say, the past is like a foreign country where things are done and said differently.*

Bok: From the Romany language and simply meaning 'luck', but used in Portsmouth in a negative form to mean the act of bringing bad luck or the person who brings it. My dad claimed my sailor uncle was a bok for Portsmouth FC as they always lost when he was in port and went to Fratton Park.

Brahma: There are various spellings but only one pronunciation for this word, which can be used as a noun or adjective. Broadly, it means something or someone of outstanding quality, as in 'What a brahma ruby' (*see below*) or 'She's a right little brahma.' Unlikely, I would have thought, but it may have some connection to the impressive bull of that name. One of the three major deities in the Hindu pantheon bears this name, which may also have some bearing on the matter.

Cushdy: Another Romany expression, broadly meaning 'good'. You might make a cushdy bargain, or say that someone has had a cushdy result. Sometimes the word is used on its own in reaction to hearing of someone's good fortune, as in 'Did you hear about Baggy? He's moved in with that brahma-lookin' nympho widow who owns a pub.' An appropriate response would be: 'Yeah? Cushdy...'

Dinlow: Fool, idiot. Often used in the short form of 'din', and can also be used as an adjective as in 'You dinny tosser.' I am told this is yet another Romany word with common currency in Portsmouth.

Iron: A gay man. One half of the rhyming slang 'Iron hoof' for 'poof'. Other and seemingly limitless non-pc allusions included shirt-lifter and turd burglar. Lesbians may be referred to as muff-divers or minge-munchers or even carpet biters. There is a well-loved if apocryphal tale that, in the 1970s, an anonymous wag took a small ad in the For Sale section of Portsmouth's daily newspaper. The clearly naive young lady who took the call duly typed it up and it appeared next day as follows: For Sale: One muff-diver's helmet. Only slightly used. The lovely thing was that her bosses could not reprimand the staff member who took the call for not knowing such an improper expression.

Lairy: This is a very common way of describing an irritating and sometimes aggressive general attitude, as in 'he's a lairy bastard.' Alleged to originate from mid -19th century cockney 'leery', and said to be common to south of England, particularly coastal areas.

Laitz: A state of absolute rage, as in 'he went absoloootly laitz, didn't 'e?'

NB: *Another London-esque linguistic custom in Portsmouth is to end statements with a question, as in 'I've gone down the road to see the mush, 'aven't I, and he's only done a runner, 'asn't 'e?' Origin unknown.*

Muller: To murder, but used mostly in a benevolent setting as in 'I could muller a pint'. Allegedly, the expression derives from the name of one Franz Muller, who committed the first murder on a British train when he killed and robbed Mr Thomas Briggs, a banker, on the Brighton Railway in 1864. Muller was hanged later the same year in one of the last public executions at Newgate prison in front of a mostly drunken crowd said to number 50,000. The murder resulted in the introduction of corridors to link railways carriages and the establishment of emergency communication cords. Again, the expression is said to be common to the South coast.

Mush: (pron. 'moosh'): An address to any male friend, stranger or enemy, to be used as in 'Alright, mush?' to a mate, or 'What you looking at, mush?' to someone you would quite like to hit. Again said to come from Romany, and is now somewhat dated and generally being replaced with greetings to friends and strangers by 'mate'. 'Mater' may be used with a particularly close friend. 'Matey' has more or less disappeared, but was for hundreds of years reserved for people who worked in the Naval Base, as in 'Dockyard matey.'

Oppo: A naval term for a close friend. According to the most likely source, it is short for 'opposite number' and referred to the man on board who did the same job as you during another watch. It paid to become friends for all sorts of reasons.

Pawnee: Rain. Corruption of Romany parni for 'water' and pani for 'rain'. Allegedly also from the old Gujarati word for water, picked up then corrupted by British troops in the early days of the Raj.

Ruby: Fairly modern and universally popular rhyming slang for 'curry'. Derived from Ruby Murray (1935-96), a husky-voiced Belfast-born songstress at the peak of her fame in the late 1950s.

Scran: Food. Credited generally to the RN via Liverpool or Newcastle, but also said to derive from Romany.

Shant: As with skimmish (see below), a noun or verb referring to ale or beer. Some Scots claim it as their own, others attribute it to the Royal Navy.

Shoist: Free, gratis. As in 'How much was your car?' 'Shoist, mater - I nicked it.'

Skate: Any Royal Naval rating. The term allegedly comes from the 18th century practice of nailing a fish of that name to the mainmast on long voyages for use by the crew in the absence of any obliging females on board (the genitals of the skatefish are said to be very similar to those of the female human).

Skimmish: Alcoholic drink, but usually confined to beer. Apparently peculiar to Portsmouth, but origin unknown.

Spare: Apart from the obvious, this word has two main uses. A 'bit of spare' is an available single female. To 'go spare' is to lose one's temper in an explosive manner.

Sprawntzy: Smart, well turned-out and confident-looking. Origin not known, but 'sprawny' is Polish for efficient or self-assured.

Squinny: Once again, a word which can be used as a noun or a verb or adjective. You can squinny or *be* a squinny. Basically it means whinge or whine about something in particular, or to generally be a moaner. According to academic sources it is a derivative of the word 'squint' and came into common use in the Middle Ages, but I am not convinced.

Wheee: According to decades of research (by me) this word/expression is absolutely unique to Portsmouth. As 'Well I never' might be employed in more refined circles, 'wheee' is brought in to play as a reaction to any piece of information or gossip from the mildly surprising to the truly shocking. Thus it would be used in the same way but with a different level of emphasis if someone said their bus was late that morning, or the next-door neighbour had formed a satanic circle and taken to keeping goats in the back garden for sacrificial and other purposes. I have asked people from all across the country, Britain and the world to try it out, but they can never replicate the depth, subtlety and variety of meaning conveyed by a true Pompeyite saying 'Wheee...'

Yonks: A long time. Like so many other examples, apparently imported into Pompey lingua franca by the RN. Some respected etymologists claim it comes from 'donkey's years'.

Acknowledgements

When I began my research, I planned to give credit to everyone who responded to my on-line queries and about their memories of Portsmouth in the 1950s and 60s. In practice, the list contained more than three hundred names before I even got close to the finishing line. All those kind enough to respond to my surveys and volunteer details will know who they are and my sincere thanks to you all. Photographs have been credited where possible, and a special mention is owed to George Langton, old school mate and local historian. Finally, there's the creator and devoted guardian of Memories of Bygone Portsmouth, JJ Marshalsay:

Memories of Bygone Portsmouth
https://www.facebook.com/groups/36600555020 1426/

Other sources include:

Portsmouth Past and Present:
https://www.facebook.com/groups/14298372039 69076/members/

History in Portsmouth - The Cooper Allen Music Archive
http://historyinportsmouth.co.uk/events/cooper-allen/1949.htm

A brief History of Southsea by Tim Lambert
http://www.localhistories.org/southsea.html

The Portsmouth History Centre
https://discovery.nationalarchives.gov.uk/details/a?_ref=42

The Popular Music Portsmouth Scene
http://michaelcooper.org.uk/C/pmsindex.htm

A Tale of One City
http://www.ataleofonecity.portsmouth.gov.uk/gallery/

According to one website, there are precisely ninety-seven novels and non-fiction works about or set in Portsmouth. Make that a round hundred, as the list does not include the first three of the Inspector Mowgley Murder Mystery series, written by no other than me.

The list can be found here:

https://www.mappit.net/bookmap/places/341/portsmouth-england-gb/

One of the books is 'Pompey', by Jonathan Meades, published by Vintage Books. It deals with the same era as this memoir, and has been acknowledged as a modern masterpiece. Potential customers should be advised it is not easy reading, and was described by critics as both brilliant and disgusting. A bit like the things people say about our city, then.

Other References

http://www.localhistories.org/southsea.html

Celebrities and famous people from the City of Portsmouth (welcometoportsmouth.co.uk) –

https://welcometoportsmouth.co.uk/famous-people-from-portsmouth-3.html

Portsmouth – Wikipedia
https://en.wikipedia.org/wiki/Portsmouth

And finally, everyone is entitled to their view, and here you can find some of the things the author does not like about Portsmouth. I would agree we could do without some of the listings, but we could certainly not do without the sea - and especially my dear old mate Fred Dinenage.

Why-portsmouth-sucks-a-list.html

Printed in Great Britain
by Amazon

21371352R10129